Second Chance

The Fall and Rise of John Mark

Dr John Andrews

RIVER
PUBLISHING

River Publishing & Media Ltd
info@river-publishing.co.uk

www.river-publishing.co.uk

Cover design by www.spiffingcovers.com

ISBN 978-1-908393-54-8

Printed in the UK

Contents

Dedication

Jimmy and Margaret

Mars, you have been, and continue to be, the most wonderful sister a man could have. You are generous, loyal, loving and a beautiful example of what it is to follow Jesus.

Jimmy, you became my friend, then my brother-in-law, but now you are my brother.

I love you both.
Thank you for enriching my life

Acknowledgements

To Dawn, the love of my life. You are worth far more than rubies to me. Thank you for helping me to be the man I've been called to be. I love you.

To Alan Graham, thanks for writing the foreword to this book. You are the best friend a man could have and I am blessed to be that man.

To Tim Pettingale, for your continued support, patience, guidance and encouragement and to River Publishing for helping to bring my 15th "book baby" to birth.

To the Lord Jesus, who found me, saved me, called me and has never left me. All that I am, all that I have, and all that I have achieved, is because of Your grace, loving-kindness and relentless faithfulness.

Foreword

I first met John Andrews when he was a fresh faced 17-year-old, as we were preparing to travel together to Mattersey Hall Bible College in 1984. Little did I know that our journey would blossom into a friendship that has lasted and grown stronger over almost 40 years!

I could tell you lots of stories about John, some of which might surprise you, while others might make you laugh, but the most important story to tell is that my friend John Andrews loves Jesus! This I have seen in his walk and ministry ever since we met; as he has pastored churches in Yorkshire and the Midlands of England; as Principal of our old Bible School; as he has written books and travelled the world with his wonderful, practical teaching ministry. Quite simply one can see, feel and smell that John loves Jesus.

John is a preacher of truth. He loves ministering to the saints of God wherever and whenever the opportunity arises. But he also lives the truth and is one of the most generous people I know, evidenced by the time, energy and funding he gives to the Kingdom of God.

I have so enjoyed reading the book in your hands, as it talks about the most important thing in this world: *relationships*. In its pages we read of fellowship and love, excitement and anticipation, inclusion and exclusion, falling outs, separation and hurt, forgiveness and reconciliation…

Second Chance, the Fall and Rise of John Mark has spoken significantly into my life and I believe it will cause any reader to seriously appraise their relationships and self, in the light of the great biblical challenge John brings to us. John writes in a way that keeps one wanting to read the next chapter as quickly as possible, while also needing to take time to peruse and ponder his words and enlightenment from the Scriptures.

I'm sure we will all see ourselves in the story of this marvellous uncovering of truth. John brings that truth in his own inimitable way,

with illustrations from his life and others, to shine a light onto these pages. I have cried, prayed and repented as I read, and our Lord spoke to me. What a God!

May God speak clearly through the book to you and may we, together with the writer, give glory to the God of Grace, the God of the second chance, and the God who will never leave or forsake His people.

Having walked all these years with John, I can testify that he lives what he writes. He is like John Mark, a true servant of the living God.

Alan Graham
Author of *The Good News Man*
Missionary to Zimbabwe and the World
Harare, Zimbabwe, 2022

Preface

"The greatest of all heroes is the coward who compels himself to be brave."[1]

With only nine direct references to John Mark in the New Testament, it would be easy to dismiss his story as a minor biographical insertion. Scattered across five books of the New Testament (Acts, Colossians, 2 Timothy, Philemon and 1 Peter), John Mark is afforded more words in the biblical text than most of the core twelve disciples of Jesus, yet many have missed the golden thread of this dramatic story, allowing it to be nudged and relegated to the fringe of the grand narrative of the growth and expansion of the early Church.

These few verses tell the story of a young man who, though chosen and privileged, deserted his post and his friends, was rejected by Paul, rescued by Barnabas, adopted by Peter and restored to usefulness. The "boy" who ran away eventually became the first Bishop of Alexandria, dying a horrific martyr's death in service of Jesus. The young man with the "stump fingers" became Peter's scribe and penned the first Gospel, which bears his name. The apprentice rejected by Paul as "unfit" was welcomed in by the Church and ultimately honoured by Paul as "useful". John Mark's story is one of glorious recovery and calls out to all of us who have failed by letting ourselves and others down, reminding us that we can be reclaimed, restored and re-purposed.

One of my favourite books is *Run with the Horses* by Eugene Peterson. In the commemorative edition, released after Peterson's promotion to heaven, his son Eric includes a beautiful proverbial story in the preface. In it, he tells of a young girl who would walk to the river every day and collect water for her household using two water pots, suspended from a

1. J. Sidlow Baxter, *Explore the Book*, p.217

pole across her shoulders. Though one of the pots was perfect, the other was cracked, ensuring it returned only half full each day. After some time, the cracked pot asked the little girl,

"Why do you keep using me when all I do is leak? Why don't you replace me with a new pot?"

The girl responded,

"Have you seen the beautiful flowers that grow along the path between the house and the river, and have you noticed that they only grow on *your* side of the road when we walk home?"

She continued,

"Every spring I plant seeds only on *your* side, knowing that you will water them as we walk together. These are the flowers that I pick, so our home is filled with fragrance and beauty."

The little girl concluded,

"I couldn't do it without you. What you thought was a flaw is actually a gift to us all."[2]

Second Chance is John Mark's testimony – the story of a man deemed by some as cracked beyond repair, but whose account of the life of Jesus now fills the world with fragrance and beauty. *Second Chance* is the hope of everyone who has tried and failed, who has started on the journey only to stumble along the path, and who began with passionate enthusiasm only to experience the emptiness of defeat.

To ignore these nine verses would be like ignoring the Gospel itself, for his story does not represent a subtext but the very heart and pulse of the main text. *The Fall and Rise of John Mark* is a message of hope for us all, where jars of clay once deemed useless can, through the power of grace and truth, find usefulness again.

Dr John Andrews
February 2022

1. A Promising Beginning

"When this had dawned on him, he went to the house of Mary the mother of John, also called Mark, where many people had gathered and were praying."
(Acts 12:12)

"When Barnabas and Saul had finished their mission, they returned from Jerusalem, taking with them John, also called Mark."
(Acts 12:25)

In the lottery of life, it seems like some people are born luckier than others. The opportunities afforded to them are less to do with their personal endeavour or brilliance and more to do with the context into which they were born or the community in which they grew. Though every person must take responsibility for their own character and choices, some people get the sort of start in life that significantly improves their chances of success. John Mark was one of those! Long before he realised, understood or appreciated it, John Mark was a citizen in a land of possibility. Where many had to bang on doors in the hope of creating an opportunity for themselves, for John Mark, opportunity knocked on his door and came looking for him.

Viewing his life and ours through a biblical lens, my conviction is that human existence is not a lottery, nor are our lives at the mercy of random luck, fluke or chance. As I look back on my own life I can conclude, like Paul, that the Lord has "set me apart from birth and called me by His grace",[1] and that my life has been enriched through extraordinary opportunity afforded to me. In following Jesus, I have had the privilege of travelling to many nations of the world, seeing and

1. Galatians 1:15

experiencing many wonderful things, while meeting and working with some incredible people.

All of this *blessing* has fuelled a reflection within me: *what would my life have looked like had I been born in a different place, with different people and a different perspective?* Of course, these are questions that cannot be answered and maybe should not even be asked, but as I've ruminated on what may have been, it has helped sharpen my appreciation and gratitude for what I have, however imperfect that may be. Whether opportunities have found me, or I have discovered them, as a follower of Jesus I realise I am called to make the most of them, by redeeming each of them for the glory of God.

Along with the passage they are found in, the first two of the nine "John Mark verses" highlighted in this chapter reveal six dynamic opportunities afforded to this young man, just because of the house he found himself in. Each are worthy of note and consideration in the light of the journey John Mark would eventually make.

1. He grew in a house of faith

"… *he* (Peter) *went to the house of Mary* the mother of John, also called Mark, where many people had gathered *and were praying*." (Acts 12:12)

In a beautiful double emphasis this verse highlights the fact that Mary's house, (John Mark's father is never mentioned), was a house of faith. Of all the places Peter could have gone, when he realised he wasn't dreaming and had actually been delivered from prison, he decided to go there. Furthermore, when he got there, we are told that many had gathered to pray. For followers of The Way in 1st Century Jerusalem, this was a well-known house, perhaps part of a network of other homes and dwellings scattered across the city. There is even a suggestion by some that this may have been the place in which Jesus held His final Passover – a house with a "large upper room, furnished and ready",[2] but

2. Mark 14:15

there is no hard evidence to back up such a theory (even though it is a cool one). Last Supper or not, Mary's house was a significant meeting place for believers and Peter knew exactly where it was. Factor into this Mary's nephew, a man introduced to us earlier in the book of Acts as Joseph a Levite from Cyprus, renamed and better known as Barnabas, and it is apparent that not only Mary, but members of her wider family had been dramatically impacted by Jesus and were active followers of The Way. [3]

2. He lived in a house of courage

"He (Herod) had James, the brother of John, put to death with the sword. When he saw that this met with approval among the Jews, *he proceeded to seize Peter also*." (Acts 12:2-3)

Chapter 12 begins with the brutal execution of James, the first of Jesus' original twelve disciples to be martyred, followed by the arrest and imprisonment and probable execution of Peter. After Stephen's death at the hands of his opponents, the believers in Jerusalem had scattered throughout Judea and Samaria, but it seemed the Apostles stayed, enabling the church to stabilise, rebuild and flourish once again.

This fresh wave of persecution under Herod was motivated more by political expediency than religious conviction, but once again the believers in Jerusalem found themselves under threat. Yet, with one apostle dead and another in prison, Mary opened her home as a place of worship, encouragement and prayer-filled resistance to the fear and intimidation rife in the city, literally putting her home and family on the line for Jesus.

Later when penning his Gospel, Mary's son would recall and record the words of Jesus as He prepared His young followers for their future:

"All men will hate you because of Me, but he who stands firm to the end will be saved."[4]

---

3. Acts 4:36-37 and Colossians 4:10
4. Mark 13:13

In the midst of the hatred, Mary stood firm and built a house of courage!

3. He benefited from a house of wealth

There are clues within this chapter and beyond that suggest Mary may have been a woman of significant financial means:

"... the house of Mary..." (Acts 12:12)

If we accept that Mary owned the house in question, then she is a house owner within the city of Jerusalem, a material privilege few at that time would have been able to enjoy.

"... where *many people* had gathered..." (Acts 12:12)

We are not sure how many is *many*, but the text highlights the fact that this was more than a few. The implication is of a significant group and thus it was a house big enough to accommodate them all.

"Peter knocked at the *outer entrance*..." (Acts 12:13)

Some translations have "door of the gate or gateway". A *pulṓn* was a large door or gate at the entrance of a building or city, and in this specific case probably indicates a gated entrance from the street, opening to a passageway leading through to an inner court. This was a house of substance.

"... and a *servant* named Rhoda came to answer the door." (Acts 12:13)

The word used here is *paidískē* which can point to either a young girl or female servant or slave, explaining the difference in some translations. If Rhoda was a servant, and not just one of the young women in the prayer meeting, this is another strong clue as to the wealth of the home.

"Joseph a Levite from Cyprus... *sold a field he owned* and brought the money and put it at the apostles' feet." (Acts 4:36-37)

Remember, Barnabas is John Mark's cousin. From this it seems that not only was this a family of faith, but a family of means.

If these are dots we are willing to connect, then John Mark would have benefitted from the opportunities that wealth can create, and in his world no benefit would have been greater or more sought after than a good education. In a world where education was the privilege of the few and where illiteracy the more common experience of the masses, wealth ensured that the young man we meet in Acts 12 was probably already able to read and write in more than one language.

His name hints at this, with John a Jewish name and Mark a Roman name (one of the most popular in Roman society at the time). With wealth, and a name that reflected both Jewish and Roman orientation, John Mark, I would suggest, was fluent in Aramaic (the everyday language of Israel), Latin (the language of Rome) and Greek (the dominant working common language for the Hellenised world). The benefit of wealth afforded him the privilege of education.

4. He experienced a house of miracles

"But Peter kept on knocking, and when they opened the door and saw him, they were astonished. Peter motioned with his hand for them to be quiet and *described how the Lord had brought him out of prison*." (Acts 12:16-17)

What a story this must have been to hear direct from Peter's mouth! Though the prayer gathering struggled to come to terms with what Rhoda was saying – "Hey, I think Peter is at the door!" – they were soon silent, transfixed and enthralled as Peter unpacked the details of his eventful night. Imagine hearing such a thing and imagine having such a man in your house! John Mark had a front row seat to one of the greatest acts of personal deliverance in the history of the Jerusalem church. James was dead, but Peter now sat right in front of the young man, very much alive. Hearing of miracles is one thing, but seeing them for yourself is something else. This must have been a moment when John Mark's faith, courage, confidence and expectations rose to new levels. The God he served not only opened the Red Sea and the Jordan River, He could open graves and prison doors.

5. He enjoyed a house of credibility

"'*Tell James and the other brothers and sisters about this*,' he said, and then he left for another place." (Acts 12:17)

It's so easy to miss this powerful little detail as we rush to the end of the story, but notice that Peter, a senior leadership figure in the church at Jerusalem, leaves it to those present at Mary's house to pass on the story of his deliverance. We don't know who was in charge that night or who was leading the prayer meeting, maybe it was Mary herself, but Peter trusted them enough, and their reputation among the believers was such, that they were given the task of conveying the news, not just generally to the believers, but specifically to James, a man (the half-brother of Jesus) who at the time was clearly emerging as a serious shepherd and leader of the church.[5] Mary's house, the home of John Mark, was not only the first place Peter thought of going when he escaped from prison, but was now the emissary of the apostle himself.

Such credibility doesn't just happen overnight but is built over time and it seems that Mary's house, over years of church growth and prosperity, and in the difficult times of opposition and persecution, proved both a trustworthy haven of the saints and a herald of the message!

6. He was discipled in a house of service

"When Barnabas and Saul had finished their mission, they returned from Jerusalem, *taking with them John, also called Mark*." (Acts 12:25)

If we read back into Acts chapter 11, we see Barnabas ministering in Antioch, a largely gentile context, and while there, he goes in search of Saul, later known as Paul the apostle. The text puts it so beautifully:

"Then Barnabas went to Tarsus to look for Saul, and when he found him, he brought him to Antioch." (Acts 11:25)

Barnabas and Saul ministered there for a further year before bringing a gift of aid to the believers in Judea from Antioch, hence the reason they are now back in Jerusalem. Note the echo of Acts 11:25 in these words:

"... they returned from Jerusalem, taking with them John, also called Mark."

Just as Barnabas had returned to Antioch with Saul, so now both men return to Antioch with John Mark. My belief (though I won't argue too hard from silence) is that Barnabas is the one initiating this invitation and Saul was happy to go along with it. This might also be a factor as to why both men disagreed so passionately over John Mark's continued involvement in Acts 15. But we'll return to that episode in a later chapter.

At this moment in the story, it seems clear that just as Barnabas found Saul, deeming him important for the cause and ready for service, I assume the same principles are guiding the decision to take John Mark. The son of Mary, I suggest, was already serving the church and showing enough character and gift that two mature activists decided to take him with them, because he was a servant raised in a house of service. On such trips there was no place for sentiment, for they knew that every step of the journey would be tough and require much from the young man, but clearly they saw enough in him to take the risk and offer him the opportunity of being part of the mission beyond the boundaries of Jerusalem. Had Barnabas and Saul not believed he was ready, they would not have taken John Mark along.

What a start the young man seemed to have. We, of course, have the benefit of looking back on John Mark's life from the security of knowing the end of his story, but he was living it, and what might seem obvious to us from our vantage point, may not have seemed so clear to him. What looks like a glorious God-ordained opportunity from the comfort of our armchairs, may have been completely missed by him in that moment. So, as we reflect on his opportunities and the possibilities they created, how might his world speak to ours?

Lesson #1: Some opportunities are redeemed with hindsight

People say that hindsight is 20/20 vision. We can see things clearly and with a better understanding when we look back. But my response to that idea is "maybe… sometimes… not always". Looking back is no guarantee that we will see anything with more clarity, especially if the lens through which we look is damaged or obscured. Hindsight can be a powerful tool to help us move forward, but only when we as followers of Jesus look with eyes tempered by humility and changed by truth.

Hindsight can become foresight when we look through redeemed eyesight!

Looking back is no guarantee of 20/20 vision, rather it is *how* we look back that can determine whether an opportunity from our past is truly dead or merely dormant. Clearly there are opportunities that come and go, and once gone they never come again, but I want to suggest to you that there are some opportunities that come our way but never go. Rather, they become dormant until awakened by redeemed eyes, thus helping us to see what was, in the light of what now is.

Later John Mark would write these magnificent words:

"The beginning of the gospel of Jesus Christ, the Son of God." (Mark 1:1)

His words are accepted by many as the first recorded words of the life and ministry of Jesus, the first Gospel, of which Matthew, Luke and John are the other three. John Mark grew up in Jerusalem, surrounded by first wave, eye-witness followers of Jesus. He clearly knew many of the early founding apostles personally, including James and Peter. He lived in a house that may even have entertained Jesus personally, and he travelled with Barnabas and Saul/Paul. All of these opportunities would have simply been enjoyed and lived, part of his experience as a follower of The Way. However, when he came to write the account of Jesus, suddenly looking back with redeemed eyes, his hindsight becomes a voice of foresight that will speak to billions across the earth for generations to come. The opportunities granted to John Mark as he just got on with his life weren't missed, they simply lay dormant, waiting for the moment when they would be liberated by purpose-redeemed vision!

Follower of Jesus, can I encourage you to *look back*?

There may well be opportunities in your past that have come and gone, never to return. But there may be some deposits of grace in your past that haven't gone, but are simply waiting to be awakened to the purpose for which they were intended. If we are prepared to look back into our past with redeemed eyes, we may see opportunities that aren't dead but dormant, and through a purpose-redeemed vision, can spring to life again.

Hindsight can become foresight when we look through redeemed eyesight!

Lesson #2: Some opportunities can be hidden in plain sight

It is so easy to miss stuff that is right in front of us. This happens because sometimes we're just not paying attention, or we are distracted, it doesn't fit with our plans or we don't deem it important enough to notice.

When Barnabas and Saul showed up at John Mark's house, that was an opportunity virtually impossible to miss, a moment when he, a relative novice, was invited onto the team of two incredibly gifted men. Of the six opportunities John Mark had, this is clearly the stand-out winner, right?

Therein lies the problem and the challenge. While waiting and hoping for the *big opportunity*, the stand-out "destiny" moment, John Mark was in danger of missing and undervaluing the *hidden in plain sight opportunities* that were all around him: those routine old prayer meetings his mother hosted, the courage to open up her home when persecution was rife, the fact that Peter knew where he lived and had clearly visited before, and the reality that his home was a place of faith, generosity, service and influence. As we look back it's easy for us to see and appreciate what John Mark may have missed, because it was hidden in plain sight, just a normal routine part of his world; an everyday experience.

The ordinary is often the vehicle for opportunity!

Follower of Jesus, can I encourage you to *look around*?

I urge you to invest some time into considering the ordinary and the routine of your world. Is it possible that God-sent opportunities are hidden within the ordinary of your everyday; in the relationships and rhythms of your week or even within the confines of your job or primary responsibilities? The danger is that if we're waiting for a "Barnabas" to show up, then we might miss a whole stack of glorious life-enriching opportunities hidden under the dust of the familiar and the disguise of the ordinary.

Had I been transported back in time into John Mark's world, I would have tried to show him that his ordinary life was pretty special and some of the things in danger of being hidden in plain sight were in fact glorious, God-sent, heaven-shaped opportunities. My granny used to say that "familiarity breeds contempt". If for some of us, contempt is too strong a word and doesn't describe our experience, I do know that in my life familiarity has bred *complacency*. Contempt may be the offspring of complacency, but my experience has taught me that if I allow complacency to take up residence in my thinking, it can be just as destructive and deeply damaging to my world.

The ordinary is often the vehicle for opportunity!

Lesson #3: Some opportunities are created by others but enjoyed by us

In August 2021, I enjoyed watching the Summer Olympic Games held in Tokyo. These should have been held in 2020, but due to the global pandemic created by the outbreak of Covid19, over a year of lockdown was endured by most of the world, including the athletes. Great Britain did pretty well, winning 65 medals of which 22 were gold, 21 silver and 22 bronze. However, what struck me was the pattern when the athletes were interviewed. Virtually every GB medal winner spent time thanking and mentioning family, coaches, support staff and their sponsors. Few talked about themselves, most talked about those who had helped them achieve their goal of getting to and medalling at the Olympics.

Some opportunities we make but most we take

I understand and accept the premise that sometimes we have to go out and make something that isn't there and create for ourselves an opportunity that, if we wait, will never come. The last thing I want to do is blunt anyone's enthusiasm to go out into the world and create and make something amazing. However, I do want to highlight the fact that, in most cases, we get to *take* our opportunities because someone, or a combination of "someones", be they human or divine, helped *make* them for us.

John Mark got to take the opportunity to go to school because someone's wealth made the way.

John Mark got to take the opportunity to grow in faith because his mother worked hard to make an environment of faith in which he grew.

John Mark got to take the opportunity to go with Barnabas and Saul because they made the way possible by extending an invitation.

John Mark got to write great stories down because others lived them and told them.

When I think of my own life, I'm very conscious of this magnificent tension. I fully understand and accept that certain things happened because I made them happen, but I am deeply aware that the vast majority of what I have, what I've achieved and received, has not been because I made it happen, but because I took the opportunities that others intentionally or unintentionally created for me.

Some opportunities we make but most we take

Follower of Jesus, can I encourage you to *look forward*?

Could it be that there are opportunities waiting for you because others have invested in you, or that an invitation is being extended to you that is less about what you have made and more about what others, including the Lord have created? Nowhere in the Scriptures did one person make it on their own, nor were they left to make every opportunity for themselves. The narrative of Scripture repeats over and over the idea that it takes a "we to make a me", and that *John Marks* get to "become" because of divine investment and community commitment.

We don't have to stand alone and make it, rather we can learn to stand together and take it. As you look forward, dare to believe that you will benefit from the generosity and grace of others. As you look forward, be open to the Marys, Barnabas', Sauls and Peters who will collide with your world. The Lord sees you, He knows you, and He understands exactly what and who you need. John Mark became a bigger, better man in part because of the people who helped him "become". They have been there… they are there… they are waiting.

Opportunities are not always obvious, but they are there. It is easy to look at John Mark and compare our lives and bemoan our lack. Each journey is different, and no two experiences are the same, but I believe in the Lord of opportunity, for He is also the God of possibility. Perhaps, encouraged by John Mark, we can take a fresh look at our lives through the lens of grace and truth. As we *look back*, maybe that which is dormant will spring to life. As we *look around*, perhaps the opportunity hidden in the ordinary will be revealed. As we *look forward*, we will receive a harvest of that previously invested and get to take what others have worked so hard to make.

The Lord of possibility will create the moments of opportunity.

Time for Reflection

As you look back on your life, what experiences or factors do you now see as opportunities, which didn't seem like opportunities at the time? For John Mark we saw six, how many can you list?

Look back
"Hindsight can become foresight when we look through redeemed eyesight." As we look at our lives through a Jesus lens, what dormant opportunities have or could come to life again?

Look around
"The ordinary is often the vehicle for opportunity." Consider the shape of your world right now. What everyday experiences might be the opportunity for you to excel?

Look forward
"Some opportunities we make but most we take." Are there benefits in your world now that are the harvest of someone else's investment? How might understanding this impact our attitude and actions?

2. Embracing Your Place

"When they arrived at Salamis, they proclaimed the word of God in the Jewish synagogues. John was with them as their helper."
(Acts 13:5)

It's not easy to fit in at the best of times, but imagine trying to fit in with Barnabas and Saul. The glorious opportunity afforded to John Mark carried with it a sizeable challenge – that of learning to work for and with two outstanding men. Barnabas may have been a relative, but his pastoral reputation was well established by now among the followers of The Way, soon to be named as an apostle.[1] As for Saul, his scholarly expertise was already well developed, something Barnabas had taken full advantage of when he invited Saul back to Antioch to teach the believers there for a year.[2] Even before his conversion to Jesus, Saul's red hot relentless zeal went before him which, it seems, the call to follow Jesus had only intensified. Arriving in Antioch, perhaps John Mark imagined this would be home for a while, but soon he found himself on the road with two men *set apart* by the Holy Spirit and *sent off* by the church into an unknown, unexplored world as far as the message of Jesus was concerned. John Mark had gone from a place of relative comfort and ease to being on the front line of missional expansion into the Gentile world.[3]

But why was he there? Why had they taken him along? John Mark's initial role alongside Barnabas and Saul is captured succinctly for us by Dr. Luke in Acts 13:5:

"... John was with them as their *helper*."

The word translated helper here is *hupērétēs* and comprises two

1. Acts 14:14
2. Acts 11:25-26
3. Acts 13:1-5

words, namely, *hupó* meaning "under" or "beneath" and *erétēs* meaning "a rower". Literally, John Mark is described as an *under-rower*, a word carrying with it the idea of a servant, attendant, subordinate or general assistant.

In both his gospel and the book of Acts, Luke makes use of this word on three occasions that reflect on how John Mark is described:

"Just as they were handed down to us by those, who from the first were eyewitnesses and *servants* of the word." (Luke 1:2)

"Then He (Jesus) rolled up the scroll, gave it back to the *attendant* and sat down." (Luke 4:20)

"Now get up and stand on your feet. I (the Lord) have appeared to you to appoint you as a *servant* and as a witness of what you have seen and will see of Me." (Acts 26:16)

We can't be sure what John Mark's day to day duties looked like, but what is certain is that his role was one of servant, attendant and assistant to Barnabas and Saul. Undoubtedly opportunities to teach, proclaim and minister would come his way, but his primary job description of *under-rower* meant that he had to learn to row on someone else's ship!

By the time Barnabas, Saul and John Mark set sale on their epic first missionary journey in approximately AD47, the Roman Navy was established as a powerhouse of logistical and military support in both the expansion and consolation of the Empire. Two major fleets were based in Italy itself (with other provincial fleets strategically positioned around the Roman world). Misenum, on the northern shore of the bay of Naples, was home to the main fleet, and by AD69 housed some 10,000 men and a fleet of 50 ships. The second Italian fleet was stationed at Ravenna on the Adriatic Sea on the Po River and was home to about 5000 personnel.[4] One glance at any of these great ships as they patrolled the Mediterranean or Adriatic seas would leave the observer in no doubt as to the importance, influence and power of an *hupērétēs*.

4. carolashby.com/the-roman-navy/

John Mark had been invited onto Barnabas and Saul's ship and then immediately escorted below deck, handed an oar and told to row. As important, influential and potentially powerful as such a role was, it was nonetheless *below deck*. If he was to not merely survive the opportunity but thrive in it, then John Mark had to move from tolerating the position of *under-rower* to celebrating it. It would not be enough to simply row; his was the call to *become* an under-rower, embracing his place as unto the Lord.

Was this what John Mark had expected? Had he anticipated or even wanted to be on a boat to Cyprus? Was he ready to serve two demanding men? As he gripped his oar, he faced a daunting and difficult challenge. He was being asked to be an *under-rower*, but was he ready and willing to embrace his place?

Over years of ministry in the church, I have seen many people grip the oar and struggle with it. As I've observed their battle, the issue has rarely been about their ability to row, but more often about their mentality as a rower. Embracing a place where we did not expect to be, and serving it as though it was our first choice, is one of the greatest challenges we will ever face. The tension between where we hoped to be and where we actually are, can be so overwhelming that many simply let go of the oar and abandon ship.

Sometimes we find ourselves *below deck*. We're on a great ship, surrounded by good people, but the place we've been asked to embrace wasn't part of the plan. How we react in such moments can determine whether the role of *under-rower* becomes purposeful or purgatorial; an experience that is life-enhancing or soul-destroying.

As a teenager with the call of God on my life, I was keen to serve that call by volunteering in my local church. I was handed a sweeping brush by an elderly deacon and *asked to row*.

As a budding preacher, I was keen to exercise the gift the Lord had given me, hoping for many pulpit opportunities. I was handed a Sunday school class of young teenagers and *asked to row*.

When I was ready to leave Bible College and show the world what they had been missing, the Lord handed me to a dozen people in a tiny Yorkshire village and *asked me to row.*

In truth, I didn't plan for these oars and, left to my own devices, probably would not have picked any of them, but they were handed to me, and with them the call to embrace my place as an *under-rower* on someone else's ship. For each of these oars I had enough ability, but the Lord already knew that. The issue wasn't my ability but my mentality. The question wasn't "could I do it?" but rather "did I want to do it?" I learned through these experiences, and many more like them, that *anyone can row but not everyone becomes a rower*!

Without reading too much into the text, I believe this is the challenge facing John Mark. History shows us that his ability was not in question, but now, the young man who had enjoyed a life of relative privilege, sits below deck with no control over the destination and no say in the program. He's been asked to just row.

Do you feel like you are below deck and yet you know the Lord is with you?

Is there an oar in your hand that you didn't expect to be holding, yet you know somehow the Lord put it there?

If your answer is yes to these questions, then your focus should not be on getting above deck or swapping out your oar. Instead, you should focus on another question: How do I embrace the place of *under-rower*?

Serve out of choice and cause

There is a common misconception that Roman Naval ships were propelled by slave-power below deck. While this may have been true of commercial vessels, it wasn't true of the Roman Navy. In fact, just like a legionary or auxiliary soldier, those working on Roman ships were free men who had voluntarily enlisted. If someone signed up to enlist in the Navy, they submitted to a twenty-six year term of service, with the promise that if they survived their service period, they would have Roman citizenship conferred upon them.[5] In theory, at least, every man on board ship, whether above or below deck, was there by choice, each having potentially committed over a quarter of a century to the cause of Rome. As their battle ships cut through the waves to help impose the will of Rome across the earth, they were powered by free men who wanted to be there! Whenever the going got tough for these men they remembered, *Choice and Cause.*

John Mark was invited by Barnabas and Saul to be part of a cause much greater than himself. How much of that he understood when he agreed and signed up is impossible to tell, but I cannot imagine that before he left home the glory of the cause and the grit of the journey was not clearly explained to him. Knowing Barnabas and Saul as we do from the text, they would have wanted their young helper to be well informed and in no way misled. John Mark knew what he was getting into. It is not inconceivable that what he thought he was signing up to and what he actually experienced were two different things, but the choice remained his and the cause remained unchanged. When he said yes, Barnabas, and most certainly Saul, accepted this as an indication that John Mark knew exactly what he was saying yes to and therefore expected him to stick with it, no matter what. If he said yes, then as far as they were concerned, he was all in!

Later Paul (Saul) writing to the church at Philippi would reflect on the example of Jesus Himself, who made a choice for a greater cause. Paul tells us that Jesus made the choice to "make Himself nothing", to embrace the very "nature of a servant", to "humble Himself" in human form and become "obedient to death, even death on a cross."[6] As the writer to the Hebrews added, it was for the "joy set before Him" that

---

5. carolashby.com/the-roman-navy/
6. Philippians 2:6-8 (although we should understand these words in the light of the whole passage, verses 1-18

Jesus made the choice to "endure the cross" and "scorn its shame."[7] This was how Paul chose to live and this was how he expected John Mark to live.

I said yes to a greater cause in my mid-teens, but in this context, I'm reminded of two life-lessons I've learned about serving that cause.

Lesson #1: It is difficult to embrace our place when it doesn't look like how we planned

As I write these words, my life does not look how I thought it would look. Unexpected twists and turns in the road have left me with an oar in my hand that I didn't think I'd be holding. I'm still getting to serve the Lord, teach His word and use my gifts, but all of that is happening in a way I never really anticipated. Now, with this oar in my hand, I have some decisions to make. I can drop it and look for something else, I can use it badly in protest to my place, or I can embrace it and give my best to it. I've learned not to allow the oar I'm holding (which I may or may not have envisioned or wanted) to eclipse the choice I made.

Lesson #2: It is difficult to embrace our place if we cannot see a bigger picture and the greater cause

I've discovered that when I focus on the oar alone, or the place I'm sitting, that such a vision is both small and demotivating. If all I'm doing is rowing, all day, every day, and that is all I see, then I find myself falling out of love with rowing. However, when I remember that my rowing is part of a bigger machine, a bigger cause, a bigger plan, and a bigger reward, it enables me to see my role as *under-rower* in a much more empowering, life-giving way.

For the Roman crewman, it was vital to remember that although he was below deck he was part of an ever-expanding Empire. For John Mark, it was vital to remember that although he was attending to Barnabas and

7. Hebrews 12:2

Saul, he was part of a Kingdom that would outlast the Roman Empire he currently lived under. For me, for us, it is vital to remember that every time we put our oars in the water, something bigger than us is going on and something greater than us is being achieved.

Surrender personal autonomy

When someone signed up for the Roman Navy, they essentially signed their life away for twenty-six years. If they were to serve Rome and the Navy well, the *under-rower* had to leave his personal agendas, ambitions and desires at the door. I must be careful not to push this analogy so far that it takes us to a world where personal freedoms are curtailed and where *yes* is the only word expected and celebrated. Too many Christian leaders, churches and Christian organisations have used such a position to manipulate, coerce and exploit servants of God who have said yes to Jesus and His church. However, as I was wisely instructed once as a young leader, "the key to abuse is not non-use but right use", so we dare not reject the truth at the heart of this idea, for fear it will be highjacked by unscrupulous people.

At the very core of the call to follow Jesus is the acceptance of surrender:

"If anyone would come after Me, he must deny himself and take up his cross daily and follow Me." (Luke 9:23)

Paul echoes this (now there's a surprise!) when he concludes:

"...You are not your own; you were bought with a price..." (1 Corinthians 6:19-20)

Surrendering our personal autonomy to Jesus and to His cause does not mean it no longer exists, but that we chose not to draw upon it, rather allowing His word to be our final word, and His way to become our way. In some ways, that is the relatively straight forward and "easy part" of this idea, but it gets more complicated when our "followership" of Jesus needs to be expressed in our service of others. To what extent am I expected to surrender my autonomy to those I serve *under* and *with?* In Western culture, where individualism has become a prized and celebrated right, the idea of serving others through the surrender of self has become a difficult, and in some cases impossible, idea.

When John Mark said yes to Barnabas and Saul, he was to some extent saying no to himself. Though ultimately, he had the choice to stay or go, as an *under-rower* he was agreeing to let others make choices about where he went, how the mission was led, and what was required of him. If he was to truly embrace the position being asked of him, then he had to let go of some things he may have wanted or desired, for the greater good. To embrace his place, John Mark had to manage the tension of saying yes to Jesus while being an *under-rower* to His servants.

In managing my own tension in this area, there are two principles that, amongst others, have guided me practically when considering issues of surrender:

Principle #1: I cannot take hold if I do not let go

Currently, one of the members of our family is Pepperoni, a gorgeous Dachshund. I'd never seen myself as a small dog person, but I absolutely love my Sausage dogs. Yes, we have a second hound called Salami. In his old age, Pepper struggles to get up and down the stairs, so when he wants to ascend or descend, he positions himself at the bottom or top of the stairs and waits for an under-rowing human to come along and serve him.

One morning, I was taking breakfast up to our bedroom and there he was, waiting. He looked at me, then looked up as if to telepathically communicate, "Take me up, human." I found myself putting down the breakfast tray in order to pick him up and transport him upstairs. The non-dog owners are shouting "That's weird!", while all the humans owned by a dog are nodding with love and approval while whispering, "Well done, John." To pick Pepperoni up that day, I had to put something down. To serve him, I had to surrender self (although Dawn and I eventually enjoyed breakfast in bed).

There are moments on our journey when the place we're being asked to embrace can only be embraced if we're prepared to let go of something else; when to serve Jesus through others we have to surrender *self*. If, when we try to take the oar, we're holding onto everything else we want, or think we deserve, we'll never get a good grip and subsequently struggle to row well. Being a good *under-rower* not only requires clear focus, but a strong grip. To take hold we must let go.

Principle #2: If I can't say no… I don't go!

This sounds like a contradiction to what has gone before, but I don't believe that to be the case. As a boy, I said *yes* to Jesus as my Saviour and, in my mid-teens, I truly said *yes* to Jesus as my Lord, making a decision to surrender the autonomy of my life to Him – a decision I have maintained to this day. However, sometimes in saying yes to Jesus, we struggle to say no to His servants.

I was raised in a culture of honouring my elders and respecting men and women of God, so my default posture has always been *yes*. Under good leadership and an affirming healthy culture, *yes* is a dynamic, life-changing word. But where leaders are not so good and the culture becomes toxic, *yes* can become a dangerous and destructive word, vulnerable to manipulation. I have come to this conclusion, which I believe to be both biblical and healthy:

If I cannot say ***no*** *in any relationship, job, Christian community or denomination, then I just don't go.*

Anyone, or anything, outside of Jesus that demands explicitly or implicitly my unquestioning, unconditional loyalty, I will not surrender to. Surrendering doesn't mean taking out our brains or assuming things are as they seem. A truth-based, principle-led *no,* expressed out of heart of service, will test the integrity of our relationships and the trustworthiness of our organisations. Even in a surrendered life, there are moments when it is okay to say no!

Synergise with others

For Roman naval effectiveness, synergy was essential. The power of the oars was released through the synergy of the under-rowers. Thus, working in harmony with others was vital for success and victory. In the Roman *trieme* each man had his own oar with 150 rowers positioned in three banks, but in the *quinqueremes* it is thought that five men pulled one huge oar between them, forming part of a crew of 400 rowers. Whatever ship an under-rower found himself on, being a "one man band" was not an option. Only by learning to work as one could the men hope to survive a battle and achieve their goals. One man doing it his way and rowing to his own beat and rhythm could quite literally be the ruin of the whole. It was a case of synchronise or sink!

To embrace his place as an *under-rower*, John Mark would have to learn to row to the beat of someone else's drum, learning to negotiate with the challenge of moving from doing it "his way" to "our way". This is rarely easy for us humans. We like the idea of others synchronising to our way of doing things, and usually struggle when we are asked to adjust to others' ways of working. Synergy requires an honest and healthy awareness of self, of our strengths, weakness, likes and dislikes, as well as an awareness of those we work closely with. There may be moments when, because of our gifts, we lead, and others where we follow, but either way, synergy's rewards will not come easily or cheaply.

Though much could be said on the subject of synergy, in this context, I will offer two simple reflections that I believe are essential if, as an under-rower, I am to row well with others.

Reflection #1: Synergy is built on Trust

In his excellent book *The Speed of Trust*, Stephen Covey Jr. defines trust in the context of working with others this way:

"Simply put, trust means *confidence.* The opposite of trust – distrust – is *suspicion.* When you trust people, you have confidence in them – in their integrity and in their abilities. When you distrust people, you are suspicious of them – of their integrity, their agenda, their capabilities, or their track record."[8]

Without trust, synergy is impossible and progress is difficult. Covey summarises this within the book with a simple formula:

High trust = fast speed and low cost

Low trust = slow speed and high cost[9]

We've all experienced this reality, whether in our homes, offices, businesses, churches or ministries. If John Mark, Barnabas and Saul were to synergise, then they had to learn to trust one another. Any doubt in the character, competency or consistency of the other would radically impact their ability to row together.

Reflection #2: Synergy flows from Fit

I have watched the 1959 version of *Ben Hur* starring Charlton Heston quite a few times and there is one particular scene which I enjoy every time. Ben Hur, an expert charioteer, is on his way back to his home in Judea when he meets Balthasar, a wealthy Arabian sheik who is taking his quadriga to Jerusalem in the hope of defeating the Roman chariots. The sheik's quadriga was made up of four magnificent white horses, but somehow their charioteer could not get the best from them. As Ben Hur watched them run, he identified the problem: the horses were in the wrong positions, and he urged the sheik to make the changes. Balthasar followed Ben Hur's advice and then... well, why don't you watch the movie and see what happens – the 1959 version, if possible. It's still way

8. Stephen, M.R. Covey with Rebecca R. Merrill, *The Speed of Trust*, Simon and Schuster, UK, 2006, p.5

9. Covey, *The Speed of Trust*, p.13. I have inserted the high, slow, low and fast. In Covey's book these words are represented as directional arrows.

better than the remake in my opinion! There was nothing wrong with the horses, just where they were positioned. A change of position and suddenly synergy flowed between them.

Trying to synergise from the wrong place, or out of gifts that aren't ours, is extremely difficult, if not impossible. When the oar feels good and fits well in our hands, when there's a confidence that the place we're in is the place we're supposed to be, then we are more likely to give our best consistently to the task before us and to those around us. Much has been written on finding our place and living out of our shape, however it is one thing for me to know my place and be comfortable with my shape and another for others to recognise it and release it. Opportunities of synergy have been lost not because of a lack of ability, strength or courage, but because we failed to position under-rowers in the right place. When it comes to synergy, a small positional change can make a huge productive difference.

Suffering is part of the package

Before surrendering my life to serving Jesus as a teenager, I did seriously consider joining the British Army. I can't imagine what I was thinking, but as a young man wanting to see the world, it seemed like a good idea at the time. The careers pitch and adverts were great. I watched films of soldiers jumping out of planes, firing guns, marching in formation before crowds and generally having a good time. Interestingly, the possibility of going to war, being killed or injured, or killing other people was never mentioned! How clever to advertise the prospect of a wonderful career in the Armed Forces while failing to reference the main reason they exist. I suppose, "Join the Army and die" or "Become part of an elite killing machine" didn't sit as well in a school's career evening.

When a free man enlisted in the Roman Navy, he knew he was signing up to a life of both potential reward and certain suffering, as the cause of Rome demanded much blood from those who served it. Though they hoped to avoid death, each man who fought for Rome expected to suffer in one way or another, whether in the forests of Germania or the bogs of Britannia. Rome, in the days of John Mark, was an all-conquering force, but the cost was high and every under-rower knew it.

Embracing our place as an *under-rower* for Jesus, and in serving His church and cause, is the greatest privilege any human has. The rewards in following Jesus are, both in this life and the life to come, potentially staggering and we are right to highlight and celebrate such truths. However, suffering for that cause, though I pray it is not an everyday experience, is certainly part of the package. Even a casual glance at the life of Jesus, His core disciples, Paul and his team, reveals an uncomfortable pattern of suffering that calls for courage, endurance and perseverance. James tries to encourage us in the light of this reality:

"Consider it pure joy, my brothers, whenever you face trials of many kinds..." (James 1:2)

Thanks for that James.

Was John Mark ready for the suffering? Breakthrough prayer meetings in his mother's house are one thing, but the threat of having his own bones broken are another. Sailing off into the sunset with two outstanding men of God (now that's a picture to adorn the front of any career magazine), but running for your life when those same men become public enemies, is another. In saying yes to service, John Mark was also saying yes to suffering, whether he understood that or not. Perhaps, as we shall see, it was something he expected but ultimately was not what he wanted.

We are told,

"... John was with them as their *helper*."

John Mark was invited to embrace his place as *under-rower* to Jesus, Barnabas and Saul and the greatest enterprise in the history of the world. He was to learn quickly that the amazing opportunity carried with it huge responsibility; that the adventure of mission would be arduous and difficult, and though the profile of working with such great men may have stroked his ego, it would also expose him to his greatest test of character.

The life of the *under-rower* offers no short-cuts, quick fixes or easy pay-offs, but if we are prepared to embrace our place below deck, with all the challenges that entails, a life of opportunity and possibility awaits.

Time for Reflection

"When it comes to *under-rowing*, the issue isn't usually ability but mentality." What attitudes can militate against us taking the oar, and what attitudes can militate against us celebrating the oar when we take it?

What core beliefs will empower us to "let go" in order to "take hold"?

"Without trust, synergy is impossible and progress is difficult." What are the key elements that help build trust as we serve one another?

In taking the oar the *under-rower* was accepting the reality of both hardship and suffering. How will embracing this truth help us to hold onto the oar and keep rowing in the tough times?

3. On the Run

"From Paphos, Paul and his companions sailed to Perga in Pamphylia, where John left them to return to Jerusalem."
(Acts 13:13)

"Once a man starts running it is hard for him to stop." This was the conclusion of my grandfather who, as a veteran of the British Army, had fought in the Burma conflict during World War II. He rarely talked about the war and the details of what he saw or did, but I remember a story he told about a member of his regiment, who in the heat of battle ran from his men and his post and was never heard of again. His reflection carried no judgement, anger or resentment, but he spoke as an old soldier who understood that there is a *runner* in us all.

It seemed that John Mark didn't want to row any more, but instead chose to run in the opposite direction of the battle. Dr Luke is kind to the young man, describing the event with as little drama as possible: "... John left them...". But on the evidence of later events (which we'll come to in the following chapters), this was not only a significant episode for John Mark, but for everyone directly connected to it.

It all seemed to be going so well. From Antioch, the team sailed for Cyprus (Barnabas' home) and had a very successful time, proclaiming the word in the synagogues of Salamis, while in Paphos (the seat of the Roman Government on the island), combatting the work and influence of Elymas, described as a Jewish sorcerer and false prophet, and leading the Proconsul, a Gentile and the highest ranking official in a Roman senatorial province, to faith in Jesus. We are told that the Proconsul was "... amazed at the teaching about the Lord," a confirmation that Gentiles were not only open to the good news of Jesus, as already seen in Antioch, but were now ready to receive it. They sailed north-west from Cyprus to Pamphylia, then journeyed eight miles inland to Perga, where

John Mark made his dramatic decision to leave. Certainly, his timing was unusual. If he had wanted to leave, he had already missed two opportunities to do so, from the ports at either Paphos or Pamphylia, yet he journeyed all the way inland to Perga before turning back.

So why did he run?

Did something happen specifically in Perga that caused him to let go of his oar and leave, or had something been brewing in him, for which the arrival in Perga was a tipping point causing him to act? In truth we don't know for sure, as the narrative here and later remains respectfully silent, but there are a couple of hints within the text that might give us insights as to why John Mark left his place and went on the run.

Paul was in charge

Note the deliberate change in language in just a few short verses:

"Set apart for me Barnabas and Saul for the work to which I have called them." (Acts 13:2)

"From Paphos, Paul and his companions sailed to Perga in Pamphylia..." (Acts 13:13)

In the first reference, Barnabas seems to have pre-eminence, if the order of their names is anything to go by, and the suggestion that he is the leader is borne out in their first destination, Cyprus, Barnabas' home. Later when Paul and Silas go on what is known as Paul's second missionary journey, on their way to Derbe, they travel through Syria and Cilicia strengthening the churches, and in so doing, Paul would have almost certainly gone to Tarsus, his place of birth; one of the first stops on the way.[1] As they leave Antioch, Barnabas seems to be the *boss*.

This highlights the contrast in the second reference, when we are told "... Paul and his companions...", strikingly, not even "Paul and Barnabas". In Luke's record something has clearly shifted between arriving on

1. Acts 15:40-41

Cyprus and leaving it. Paul, it seems has risen to a more preeminent position. Their experience in Cyprus undoubtedly contributed to this, with Paul taking the lead in dealing with Elymas. As a scholar, trained under Gamaliel, he would have also taken the lead in teaching in the synagogues and debating the finer points of Jewish law. We recall this is probably why Barnabas brought him to Antioch in the first place, to help with the teaching of the fledgling church. It is interesting that from this moment on, Acts speaks of Paul and Barnabas rather than Barnabas and Paul, with the exception of Acts 15:12 and 25.

I don't think Barnabas would have been bothered by Paul assuming a more prominent role within the team. After all, the evidence within Acts suggests that Barnabas was a man who empowered and released others (I actually believe that he is a superb example of an Ephesians 4:11 Pastor). But maybe John Mark struggled. The two men were related and, although we can't be certain, there is a good chance that John Mark accepted the invitation to go with Barnabas and Saul primarily because of Barnabas. Added to this, Barnabas became a follower of Jesus before Paul, even introducing him to the Apostles at Jerusalem when his conversion was surrounded by suspicion.[2] If that is the case (and I admit it is a big *if*), then ill ease and discontentment may have been growing in John Mark from the moment the leadership momentum started to shift towards Paul in Cyprus. This might explain why he waits until Perga to make his final decision. Perhaps he was watching, listening and hoping that Barnabas would assume the lead.

A Gentile trajectory

While on Cyprus another significant shift occurs, highlighted for us in these words:

"Then Saul, who was also called Paul..." (Acts 13:9)

2. Acts 4:36-37 and 9:27

From this moment on the narrative moves from using Saul (his Jewish name) to Paul, (his gentile/Roman name), undoubtedly reflecting the trajectory of this new missional campaign. Although, as on Cyprus, he would always seek to take the message of Jesus to Jewish communities and synagogues first, it was clear that Paul's intention was to move aggressively into regions and cities that were predominantly Gentile, with a message of justification by faith in Jesus. Many within the church at that time believed that Gentiles could only come to faith in Jesus *through Moses*, but Paul saw Jesus as the fulfilment of the Law, concluding that the Gentiles were free from the requirements of the Law for salvation. Paul even opposed Peter's duplicity on this issue and further lamented the fact that people of the calibre of Barnabas were being "led astray" by this idea.[3] Paul's belief that "...by observing the law no-one will be justified" became the driving heart of his message to Jews and Gentiles alike.[4]

Was John Mark struggling with this? Now that Paul was in charge, he realised that this was the message at the heart of the new mission and possibly did not agree with it. He was raised in the church at Jerusalem were many held a view now opposite to Paul's. He had seen the Proconsul come to Jesus at Paphos and was happy that Gentiles were doing so, but like many others, he expected them to submit to Moses first.

Two further clues may add weight to this theory and his struggle. Firstly, just as there may be a message in the shift from Saul to Paul, so in chapter 13 of Acts, the narrative only ever refers to John Mark by his Hebrew name, not his Roman one:

"... *John* was with them as their helper." (Acts 13:5)

"... *John* left them..." (Acts 13:13)

Is the use of his Hebrew name a gentle hint of his struggle?

---

3. Galatians 2:11-13
4. Galatians 2:16

Secondly, when John leaves them he goes to Jerusalem, not Cyprus (where he may have had relatives), and not Antioch from where he was sent. Of course, Jerusalem was where his mother and home was, but it was also a "safe place" theologically; a place where his beliefs and ideas would be respected, supported and affirmed. Could it be that this young man was more comfortable being *John* than *Mark,* and with a more Jewish Jesus than one for the Gentiles? It is fascinating that on the four occasions he is later mentioned in the New Testament, outside of the Book of Acts (three by Paul and one by Peter), he is referred to as Mark, not John, suggesting perhaps that he ultimately accepted Paul's message and its call to the gentile world. But for now, this was a step too far. It was one thing for Saul to embrace his Paul, but this was not something John was ready or willing to do!

How did he run?

As we've seen, Dr Luke is kind to John Mark when describing the moment of his departure: "...John left them to return to Jerusalem." If this was the only piece of information we had on the event, then we might conclude that John Mark just left with the blessing of Barnabas and Saul to return home. The word used here is *apochōréō* and carries no meaning other than "to go from". However, a couple of years later, when Paul and Barnabas consider going on a second missionary journey together, Barnabas wanted to take John Mark again, but Paul refused to countenance the idea with the emphatic conclusion:

"...he (John Mark) had *deserted them* in Pamphylia and had not continued with them in the work." (Acts 15:38).

We'll come back to this verse, the fourth of our nine John Mark references, in the next chapter, but an important distinction must be made from this verse in this chapter. Paul does not say John Mark simply left (*apochōréō*) but rather that he deserted (*aphístēmi*), a stronger word suggesting "he went from his place" or "left his stand". This might explain Paul's strength of feeling on the matter. As a student,

Paul had been raised to argue, debate and discuss. As a scholar, and now herald of The Way, he was accustomed to people disagreeing with his opinion. He could handle disagreement, but what he could not handle was desertion! Paul called it as he saw it, and from his point of view, John Mark had abandoned his friends, his post and the mission, without an explanation or even a goodbye.

John didn't just leave, *he deserted,* and this gives us an insight into what he was going through, even if we aren't totally sure of why he deserted. For one reason or another, he felt he could not stay, and his only option was to run. The record is silent on whether he tried to express his concerns and if, in doing so, he was in some way rebuffed by Paul. Rather, the text suggests he simply got up one morning, packed his bags and left and I believe it was how he left even more than why he left that upset Paul. Two years later, Paul's sense of betrayal through John Mark's actions would be at the heart of one of the saddest fractures in the story of the early church. But we'll get to that later.

Had John Mark run before?

In the gospel John Mark penned, there is a unique story that references an unnamed young man, by inference not one of the core disciples of Jesus. As Jesus is being arrested it says:

"Then everyone deserted Him and fled. A young man, wearing nothing but a linen garment was following Jesus. When they seized him, he fled naked, leaving his garment behind." (Mark 14:50-52)

There is nothing whatsoever in the text that confirms this person is John Mark, so we cannot conclude anything with certainty from the silence. However, what a fascinating thought it is – that the young man accused by Paul of desertion may have also been there in the garden at the moment, when not only he, but every disciple of Jesus deserted their post and fled, leaving Jesus alone. If John Mark wasn't the young man streaking his way home that night, then at the very least we can see why he alone among the gospel writers included this story. John Mark understood that there is a runner in every person and he was living proof that redemption was possible, even for those who run!

I've discovered that there are different types of running – some good and some bad. On the surface they can look the same, but I've learned that the way I run can determine my direction of travel and even the destination I arrive at. One can be life-giving and the other soul-destroying. Here are three questions I've learned to ask myself when faced with the prospect of going on the run.

Question #1: Am I running *to* something or running *from* something?

The problem with *running from* something is that we never really arrive anywhere. "Getting away" can never satisfy us in the way that "arriving at" or "running to" does, and this lack of satisfaction simply fuels our ill ease and disappointment. Of course, there are times in life when *running from* is the only sensible and practical option available to us, but as a general principle of healthy, sustainable living, *running to* is the better way.

When calling His disciples, Jesus invited them *to* something:

"Come follow Me and I will make you..."

He never used fear of punishment as a motivator for discipleship, rather He understood that when a person runs toward something, they are inevitably leaving something behind – but for all the right reasons. A would-be follower running from fear does so in an act of self-preservation, which is the opposite of what Jesus wanted to achieve. Rather, Jesus wanted potential disciples to run toward Him, thus willingly leaving self behind and finding true life.

Abram ran *to* the Lord's purpose and found the land of promise, but later ran *from* famine and found himself on an unsanctioned stay in Egypt.

Jacob ran *from* his brother and became an exile for over two decades in a foreign land, but later ran *to* the Lord and experienced a transformational name change.

Moses ran *from* Pharaoh and spent a lifetime in the wilderness, before running *to* a bush that burned and his destiny as a deliverer.

It's clear that, for whatever reason, John Mark ran *from* something. He ended up in Jerusalem because that was his home, not his destination. "Jerusalem" is glorious if that's where we're meant to be, but if we're meant to be somewhere else, it can be a place of living without life. There is a runner in us all and, in truth, running from somewhere, someone or something is a relatively easy thing to do, but such running rarely takes us to peace and purpose.

Are you running *from* or running *to*?

Question #2: Am I running out of my principles or my pain?

Pain can be a powerful motivator when it comes to running. I discovered this pretty early in life while growing up in Belfast. I loved school and generally throughout my schooling career kept my head down, worked hard and was moderately popular. However, through a complete accident I found myself on the wrong side of a rather nasty bully and his gang, resulting in a rather painful public beating at his hands (he used his feet quite effectively as well, I recall). Suddenly, I didn't love school anymore and had my mother relented, I may never have returned. Each day I planned my route to avoid the areas I knew he and his cohorts would be, and the rest of the time prayed that by God's grace we would not collide. Eventually, my mother caught on to what was happening and threatened to go down to the school and "sort them out". As this was not an option for me, she gave me a piece of advice I didn't really want to hear: "Son, you're going to have to face up to him sooner or later." I was confronted with a choice to either stand on a principle or run out from a place of pain.

When something or someone hurts us, running is one of the most natural and normal things to want to do. Avoid where possible and appease where necessary, but just stay alive. The problem with this approach is that we start making decisions based on our pain, and the pain we experienced starts to shape our thinking and direction. We find ourselves pulling back from some people, staying away from certain places, and withholding our talents from opportunities we would normally relish. The pain screams, "I can't!"

Running due to a principle can, on the surface, look similar to running out of pain. We could define a principle as, *a truth that serves as a foundation for a system of belief and behaviour.* Based on that definition, while there will be many things we can and will say yes to, we will also have to say no to things, avoid certain situations, and stand up for ourselves by refusing to engage.

What distinguishes principle from pain is the truth we are prepared to build our lives on. *Am I going to build my belief and behaviour on a truth that transcends my experience, or on one created by my experience?*

Pain can create "truths" within our thinking that form strongholds of resistance to life and freedom. Principles (provided they are good ones, of course) create strongholds that lead us to life and freedom, while managing the pain we are experiencing. Pain screams "I can't", whereas principles assure me "I can". Pain narrows our options whereas principles create choices.

Did John Mark run out of principle (Moses then Jesus) or out of pain? In truth, we cannot be sure, but if he ran out of principle then John Mark was released, but if he ran out of pain he would live restricted. There is a runner in us all but if pain drives our race then we'll be shackled to what has been; if principles lead our race, we'll be able to embrace what can be!

Are you running based on principles or pain?

Question #3: Am I running towards the comfort I want and from the change I need?

If we've been on the planet more than five minutes, we know that change is natural, normal and necessary, and that we cannot get to the end of any journey in life without engaging seriously with it. Yet, we love our comfort too. I certainly do. I love my routines, my favourite chair, my peace-filled study, relaxing in my conservatory with Dawn, sleeping in a soft bed and watching TV with one of my Sausage dogs on my knee, while snuggling under a blanket. Bear Grylls I am not... though I like watching him while... you get the picture!

I'm pretty sure I'm not alone. There is nothing wrong with comfort, of course, unless it starts to get in the way of change. When the call of comfort militates against the challenge of change, we can find ourselves running from something that will bring life in the long-term, for something that satisfies us in the short-term. We humans love short-cuts and if we can find a way to change without too much cost and impact on our comfort, we'll sign up every time. However, by very definition change carries cost and disturbs comfort. This tension will always be part of our journey.

In the first two years of my Hebrew studies I had a wonderful teacher. She was not only brilliant at what she did, but she was kind, compassionate, patient and totally understanding. When I read the Hebrew text (some might say butchered it), she would listen as I stumbled over my pronunciation and looked vacantly at her when asked to explain an issue of grammar. But I loved being in her class. We were friends; she liked me and I liked her. However, due to changes in scheduling, I was told that for my third year I had to change teachers. I wasn't really happy with this but submitted to it.

My new teacher was brilliant too, but he wasn't so patient. He was much more argumentative and had a slightly more combative style, which he expected us all to love and embrace. After my first class with him I wanted my old teacher back, with her gentle ways and kind smile. But there was no way back. If I wanted to finish my course, I had to embrace the change. As I reflect on this experience, I really didn't like my new teacher very much, forever comparing him to *my friend*, but as I engaged with him, I came to appreciate his style, adjust to his expectations and rise to his challenges. In that year, there wasn't a single lesson where I felt comfortable or at ease with the relentless challenge of change he placed on us, but my learning accelerated and my confidence grew. I would not have chosen him, and I didn't really like his style that much, but looking back, I now know I needed him!

Let's face it, who would want to be on the road with Paul? If we take off our rose-coloured spectacles for a few moments, we see a totally focused, single-minded go-getting activist, who went from a persecutor of the Church to a proclaimer of The Way, without diminishing his zeal. Having met Jesus on the road to Damascus, his life was radically transformed and he was on a mission to tell the world. Paul was totally committed and expected everyone around him to be the same.

I suspect Barnabas may have had more people lining up to join his small group. He was generous, kind, patient and the sort of dad, big brother, or leader most of us would love to have. So, as Paul started to take the lead, John Mark was being asked to swap teachers halfway through his course, and suddenly what had seemed relatively comfortable for him was starting to feel like challenge and change. When asked to embrace this challenge, John Mark refused to do so, and rather than change, he quit the course altogether.

Are you running towards the comfort you want or from the change you need?

There is a runner in us all. If we're honest with ourselves, there have been moments when we've said no to the call to change because we would rather cling to the comfort of the familiar. We can criticise John Mark for doing what he did, but I get it, and to some extent I understand it, even if I'm not absolutely certain why he did it. There is a runner in us all, but as we seek to follow Jesus wherever He may lead, we must dig into why we are running, for as John Mark teaches us, why we run will determine where we end up.

Time for Reflection

What are the dangers of running from somewhere we know we should be and something we know we should be doing? Why is moving towards something a better way?

"What distinguishes principle from pain is the truth we are prepared to build our lives on." Running based on a principle and out of pain can look very similar on the surface, but what are the fundamental ideas that separate them? How do we know if we are saying "no" on the basis of principle or pain?

Comfort is what we want but change is what we need. Is there a situation in your life that is demanding positive, life-giving change, but you are running away from it? Is there any area of your life (job, relationships, community, purpose) where you have chosen comfort over change?

4. No Way Back

"Barnabas wanted to take John, also called Mark, with them, but Paul did not think it wise to take him, because he had deserted them in Pamphylia and had not continued with them in the work."
(Acts 15:37-38)

There are moments in life when, if we want to go forward, we have to go back; where our restoration is only possible if we are prepared to make restitution. As I've served the Church over many years, I've noticed our tendency to readily embrace the reality of being forgiven, but a hesitance to help repair something we had a hand in breaking. We love the idea of a clean slate and a *new day*, but we don't like the challenge of addressing our actions and their consequences from the *old day*! Too often, under the covering of cheap grace, we encourage people to "just move on", while ignoring the elephant in the room preventing them from doing so. When we ignore the *elephant,* we deny a reality that won't conveniently disappear, and we soon discover that pretending it isn't there does not make it so. When we ignore the *elephant,* we abdicate our responsibility to address our failure, or a fracture, and we soon discover that moving on does not mean we left the elephant behind!

For John Mark, *going back* was a vital factor in going forward. His journey finished when he made it home to Jerusalem, but his running did not stop. Sooner or later he would have to face the two men he left in Perga. This may have happened when Paul and Barnabas returned to Jerusalem. After completing their first missionary journey together, they stayed in Antioch for a while, where they found themselves at odds with those who believed that circumcision was essential for salvation. Both Paul and Barnabas were sent to Jerusalem by the believers at Antioch, to represent the Gentile question in what became a history-making, world-changing council. Luke is silent on whether Paul, Barnabas and

John Mark met in Jerusalem, but the fact that Barnabas felt confident enough to raise the issue of his relative rejoining the team, as they were about to leave on their second trip, may suggest that some contact was made. Whatever did or did not happen in Jerusalem, it was in Antioch where the contention around John Mark took centre stage.

"Barnabas wanted to take John, also called Mark, with them..." (v37)

Barnabas' request was prompted by Paul's desire for a return journey to the churches they had planted during their first two-year trip:

"Let us go back and visit the believers in all the towns where we preached the word of the Lord and see how they are doing." (v36)

For Barnabas, this was the ideal time to reintroduce John Mark into the conversation suggesting that, in his eyes at least, John Mark was no longer a flight risk and that Paul was potentially receptive to the idea. If John Mark had travelled from Jerusalem to Antioch with them, this would only have added to his confidence. But even Barnabas must have been taken aback by the strength of Paul's reaction over the idea:

"...but Paul did not think it wise to take him, because he had deserted them in Pamphylia and had not continued with them in the work." (v38)

This translation is quite kind. The nuance of the text suggests that Paul didn't want John Mark to go with them because he considered him "unfit" (*axióo*) for the task at hand. This explains his strength of feeling and his willingness to split with his friend Barnabas:

"They had such a sharp disagreement that they parted company..." (v39)

The word translated "sharp disagreement" here is *paroxusmós*, and points to the idea of "stirring up of anger" or an "angry dispute". The English word *paroxysm* is derived from this Greek word and is defined as "a sudden attack or outburst of a particular emotion or activity". This sudden eruption had been brewing for some time and its consequences would last for years to come. John Mark may have been ready to take his second chance, but Paul made it absolutely clear that he was not willing to give him one.

Why was Paul so resistant to the idea of taking John Mark along? Why did he react so strongly, even at the cost of his ministry partnership with Barnabas? Why did he consider John Mark unfit?

It's hard to be precise on the answer to these questions, but I think there are clues in the text that reveal the fuel that fed the fire of Paul's conclusion and contention.

John Mark deserted them

As we have already observed in the previous chapter, Dr Luke's narrative around the episode in Perga was kinder to John Mark than Paul's assessment. Luke tells us that,

"...John *left them* to return to Jerusalem." (Acts 13:13)

In Paul's eyes, John Mark did not simply leave, rather he "went from his place" and "left his stand", deserting his friends at a crucial moment during their first missionary journey. Added to this is the fact that the narrative does not record a formal apology from John Mark to both men, and that the request to have him return to the team comes from Barnabas, not from the young man himself. John Mark may well have apologised to Paul, but the fact that nothing is recorded by Luke suggests it's not in the story because it did not happen. What is clear is that John Mark's actions in Perga deeply disappointed Paul and now, two years later, his feelings had developed into disappointment in the young man himself.

Later Paul would write to the church at Philippi with the uncompromising declaration, "for me to live is Christ", describing his life as a "drink offering" being poured out, while "pressing on towards the goal to win the prize", having considered everything in his life "rubbish, that I may gain Christ."[1] For a man such as Paul, desertion was

1. Philippians 1:21, 2:17, 3:14 and 3:8

not an option! For him, anything less than 100% was unthinkable, hence in his mind there was no way back for a deserter!

John Mark discarded his responsibility

When writing to the churches, Paul often described individuals who served with him as his "fellow-workers". The word *sunergói* (*sunergós* singular), is derived from *sun* meaning "together" and *érgon* meaning "work". In fact, of the thirteen times it is used in the New Testament, twelve are attributed to Paul.[2] It is interesting then that when John Mark's actions in Perga are described, we are told that he had,

"...not continued with them in the work (*érgon*)."

John Mark's behaviour was not only the antithesis of Paul's, but represented the opposite end of the scale of the values Paul honoured the most in those around him. To be held up as one of Paul's *sunergói* was high praise indeed, and explains why Paul takes such a strong view of the young man who literally left his side and abdicated the responsibility of his work.

Later when writing to the church at Rome, Paul declared,

"So from Jerusalem all the way around to Illyricum, I have fully proclaimed the gospel of Christ. It has always been my ambition to preach the gospel where Christ was not known, so that I would not be building on someone else's foundation." (Romans 15:19-20)

Illyricum was a just a hop east across the Adriatic Sea from Italy, straddling modern nations such as Albania to the south and Croatia to the north. In other words, Paul had put in serious miles as he sought to plant churches in the regions beyond. For a man such as Paul, who saw his task as the work of advancing the cause of Jesus across the earth, it would have been hard to accept any reason why someone would abdicate such a responsibility! John Mark had rejected his *fellow-worker* privilege and Paul was reluctant to extend the invitation to such a position again.

John Mark dodged the suffering

Paul wore his suffering for Jesus like a badge of honour. When writing to the believers in Corinth (a church he helped plant but who were questioning his authority to speak into their world), he asked them to consider his suffering for Jesus as part of his credentials. Read these verses slowly:

"Are they servants of Christ? (I am out of my mind to talk like this.) I am more. I have worked much harder, been in prison more frequently, been flogged more severely, and been exposed to death again and again. Five times I received from the Jews the forty lashes minus one. Three times I was beaten with rods, once I was stoned, three times I was shipwrecked, I spent a night and a day in the open sea, I have been constantly on the move. I have been in danger from rivers, in danger from bandits, in danger from my fellow Jews, in danger from Gentiles; in danger in the city, in danger in the country, in danger at sea; and in danger from false believers. I have laboured and toiled and have often gone without sleep; I have known hunger and thirst and have often gone without food; I have been cold and naked. Besides everything else, I face daily the pressure of my concern for all the churches." (2 Corinthians 11:23-28)

When we read such a summary, it is understandable why some people weren't all that keen on joining Paul's team! Could this have been a factor in Paul's reluctance to take John Mark on their second trip? Perhaps the clue (and I hope I'm not stretching this too far), is in what happened after John Mark left them at Perga. Chapters 13-14 tell us that from Perga, Barnabas and Paul went to Pisidian Antioch where their message was well received and where,

"The word of the Lord spread through the whole region." (Acts 13:49)

From there they moved to Iconium where,

"...they spoke so effectively that a great number of Jews and Gentiles believed." (Acts 13:1)

However, it was here that trouble started to brew and on discovering a plot to ill-treat and possibly try to kill them, they fled to Lystra where they continued to preach. At Lystra, it went so well that the locals thought that Barnabas was the god Zeus and Paul his messenger, Hermes, but their celebrity status was short lived when the crowd was "won over" by opponents of the Gospel from Antioch and Iconium. How quickly the crowd turned, Luke tells us:

"They stoned Paul and dragged him outside the city thinking he was dead." (Acts 14:19).

However, I love the matter-of-factness of the narrative:

"But after the disciples gathered round him, he got up and went back into the city." (Acts 14:20)

You gotta love Paul! This is probably the "once stoned" event (once is enough for anybody), that he refers to when writing to the Corinthians, and John Mark missed all the *fun*. When Barnabas spoke on John Mark's behalf, it is entirely feasible that Paul still had scars from his Lystra experience and may have resented the fact that John Mark was nowhere to be seen when they were suffering. Writing to the church at Philippi, Paul commended one of their number, a man called Epaphroditus, someone he described as a "brother, *fellow-worker* (*sunergós*) and fellow soldier". In service to Paul, Epaphroditus' suffering was so great that he almost died, so as Paul prepared to send him back to them, he urged them to,

"...honour men like him, because he almost died for the work of Christ, risking his life to make up for the help you could not give me." (Philippians 2:25-30)

Can you see the contrast and feel the angst in Paul's heart towards John Mark? Having suffered, Paul honoured those who took up the cross of suffering with him, but he had much less tolerance for those who shunned it. It is impossible to be certain as to whether this was a factor in Paul's conclusion that John Mark was *unfit*, but the evidence seems to suggest that it was not far from his thinking. For a man such as Paul, who saw his scars as marks of service, he may have been less than impressed that John Mark had conveniently avoided the suffering and bore no scars himself.

Whether prompted by Barnabas or initiated by himself, John Mark had attempted to move his life forward by going back and addressing his fracture with Paul. Even though this was the best thing to do, the offer of conciliation and restoration was not only rejected by Paul, which would have been hard enough to take, but Paul made it clear that John Mark was *unfit* for the task at hand. As far as Paul was concerned, there was no way back for him.

Now what? What do you do when your offer is rejected? When what seemed like a good plan is thrown back in your face?

It is not too much of an overstatement to suggest that John Mark's reaction to this moment would potentially determine the trajectory of the rest of his life. Not all moments in life are equal, and there are times when the reality of rejection can either drive us toward the prison-house of pain or the possibility of purpose. Paul's decision was uncompromising in both its rationale and conclusion, but one person's opinion, however strong and considered it may be, is rarely enough to define the destiny of another person's life. Paul said "no", but what did John Mark say?

In the whole of the narrative from Acts 15:36-41, there is no record of John Mark speaking, yet from the silence, his actions speak, and perhaps the ways in which he responded carry the final word.

Response #1: John Mark did not fight Paul's opinion

As the teacher suggests,

"... there is a time to keep silence, and a time to speak." (Ecclesiastes 3:7)

Knowing when to *keep silence* or *speak* is the mark of true wisdom for sure, especially for humans who love to have the final word and love the sound of their own voice. When we are rebuked, challenged, and confronted with truths that both shock and wound us, our natural egocentric reaction is to protect and defend ourselves – even if deep down we know we are wrong and they are right. How often in desperation do we grasp for excuses to justify our position and legitimise our response?

Paul's opinion was that John Mark was a deserter and one who had abdicated his responsibility to stand with his friends and the cause of mission. It is clear that Paul believed that John Mark was unworthy of his trust. In the light of such a strong opinion, John Mark's silence might be interpreted in one of two ways: either that Paul was right in his opinion and thus he was untrustworthy, or Paul was wrong in his opinion, but such was its strength that fighting back was futile. Again, we cannot be certain which it was, but what is striking is that in the years that followed, with the growing influence John Mark enjoyed, he never once took the opportunity to correct Paul's opinion. His silence remained solid.

I find John Mark's silence deeply attractive. He could have fought back, and many would argue he should have fought back, but instead we have only silence. This I submit, is not the silence of fear, intimidation or manipulation, rather it is the silence of humility, contriteness, character and security. Regardless of who was right or wrong, John Mark concluded that silence was the best response in that instance. Sometimes our silence speaks louder than our words.

Response #2: John Mark was not put off by Paul's conclusion

To be told directly or indirectly that we are *unfit* is a body blow that some never recover from. Some words are hard to un-hear once we hear them and I'm guessing *unfit* ranks up there in the top five of that category. Words are powerful because they can journey from someone else's conclusion to our personal confession. The words people speak to us are powerful indeed, but the words we then internalise and speak *to* ourselves and *about* ourselves are both life-shaping and life-changing. This is what I believe Solomon was seeking to teach us when he wrote,

> "From the fruit of their mouth a person's stomach is filled;
> with the harvest of their lips they are satisfied.
> The tongue has the power of life and death,
> and those who love it will eat its fruit." (Proverbs 18:20-21)

Most people only ever quote verse 21, about the tongue having the power of life and death, but verses 20-21 are a couplet and together they warn us that it is *our confession* that carries the power of life and death, not the conclusions of others!

Paul's conclusion that John Mark was unfit might easily have become the young man's confession, but in the silence we see a response that suggests Paul's conclusion remained just that.

"...Barnabas took Mark and sailed for Cyprus." (Acts 15:39)

We'll dig into the fact that Barnabas *took* Mark much more in the following chapter, but I wanted to highlight one implied truth from this statement in the context of this chapter. John Mark went with Barnabas! Had John Mark believed Paul's conclusion, and had "I'm unfit" become his confession, then he would not have gone with Barnabas or anyone else. Had "unfit" been John Mark's confession, then I suggest that Acts 15 would have been the last time we heard of him, as the unfit one disappeared into obscurity. The fact that he goes with Barnabas screams to us that John Mark did not accept Paul's conclusion, and he was not put off serving the Lord because of it. Though there was no way back with Paul, nonetheless, John Mark went forward with Barnabas, and the rest as they say is history. Paul made it clear he was not for turning but in going, John Mark was making a life-shaping statement that he was not for quitting.

Time for Reflection

Why is it that sometimes going back is the only way forward? Have you ever experienced this reality? What did you do and what difference did it make?

In seeking to make things right we often ignore the principle of restitution. Though restitution is not always possible or expected, in what ways can such action be a powerful force for healing and recovery?

There are times when speaking up in our defence is the right thing to do, but sometimes silence is the better way. Why is keeping silent such a difficult and powerful thing to do?

Paul thought John Mark *unfit*. The opinions of others, especially those we love and respect, can be a stronghold in our lives. How can we ensure that the negative opinions of others do not become the defining words over our lives?

5. Second Chance

"Barnabas took Mark and sailed for Cyprus."
(Acts 15:39)

Barnabas could not have known that the simple act of taking John Mark with him would not only change his cousin's life, but would help change the world. Looking on, no one could have imagined what the *unfit deserter* would become; that the bruised boy leaving for Cyprus with Barnabas would one day become a shepherd to the broken and the author of a book that would enrich and transform the lives of billions of people. All Barnabas did was offer him a *second chance.*

It would be too easy to suggest that Barnabas' desire to offer John Mark a second chance was driven by the fact that both men were related. This would ignore a clear pattern of behaviour displayed by Barnabas from the first moment he is introduced to us in the book of Acts. Luke tells us that,

"Barnabas wanted to take John, also called Mark, with them…" (v37)

For me, the translation "wanted to take" is a little weak. The word used here is *bouleúō*, from *boulḗ*, meaning "counsel" or "will". In this context it points to the meaning, "to consult, determine, deliberate with oneself or with one another in counsel". I like the idea that Barnabas "deliberated with himself" and determined to take John Mark along. His determination was not borne out of simple family loyalty but rather was built on a strong belief system and shaped by how Barnabas saw and served others. Barnabas had a history of helping people because he believed in people, a fact Dr Luke has already clearly shown us prior to this moment. Before Barnabas and Saul engage with John Mark in Jerusalem (Acts 12), or are sent out by the church in Antioch (Acts 13:1-3), there are three major references to Barnabas in the Acts narrative.

Once we see his behaviour on these occasions, his determined actions in Acts 15 make total sense.

Son of encouragement

"Joseph, a Levite from Cyprus, whom the apostles called Barnabas (which means 'son of encouragement'), sold a field he owned and brought the money and put it at the apostles' feet." (Acts 4:36-37)

Barnabas did not sell his land to acquire more property and expand his real estate portfolio, rather he sold in order to give (behaviour that is in stark contrast to the actions of Ananias and Sapphira in Acts chapter 5). Such was his commitment to the cause of the kingdom, with an attitude of generosity towards those around him, that the apostles decided to rename him, giving him a name that more accurately reflected the man he was. They named what they saw!

Friend of Saul

"But Barnabas took him and brought him to the apostles. He told them how Saul on his journey had seen the Lord and that the Lord had spoken to him, and how in Damascus he had preached fearlessly in the name of Jesus." (Acts 9:27)

Saul had just become a follower of The Way after spearheading a violent assault against the followers of Jesus. Revolutionised by his encounter with Jesus, Saul started teaching immediately in Damascus, but after learning of death threats against him he escaped to Jerusalem and tried to join the Christian community there. However, there was understandable hesitancy.

"...but they were all afraid of him, not believing that he really was a disciple." (Acts 9:26)

Barnabas to the rescue! Note the phrase, "But Barnabas *took him*..."

This is the same word used of John Mark in Acts 15:39, only this time he's taking Saul *to* the apostles, whereas he took John Mark *with* him.[1] [2]Not only did Barnabas take hold of Saul, he stood up for him, defending him before the apostles and believers to such an extent that they accepted him and he "stayed with them". Barnabas believed in Saul so much that he risked and leveraged his own reputation in order to ensure this man was not lost to the call and cause of Christ.

Ambassador to Antioch

"News of this reached the church in Jerusalem, and they sent Barnabas to Antioch." (Acts 11:22)

When it became clear to the apostles in Jerusalem that the Lord was moving powerfully in Antioch, the third largest city in the Roman Empire, and that Gentiles as well as Jews were turning to Jesus in great numbers, they sent Barnabas. But why? Why didn't Peter and John go as they had gone to Samaria (Acts 8), and why not send James? Barnabas, of course, was from Cyprus, so he may have been a natural choice with his relative comfort with that part of the world, having lived and worked amongst Gentiles in a Hellenised context. But thanks to Dr Luke, there may be another motivator at work here. He tells us,

"He was a good man, full of the Holy Spirit and faith..." (Acts 11:24)

Barnabas was the right person for the job because "he was a good man, full of the Holy Spirit and faith". That might be why what he saw in Antioch is described as the "evidence of the grace of God" and that he was "glad and encouraged them all to remain true to the Lord with all their hearts". There is no hint of resistance to Gentiles and no hesitation to embrace that which Peter had initially struggled with.[3] Barnabas was the right person for the job because "he was a good man, full of the Holy Spirit and faith".

1. Acts 9:27 is *epilambánō*, Acts 15:39 is *paralambánō*
2. See Peter's story in Acts 10

But it doesn't end there, for Barnabas had the wisdom to realise that he could not help this expanding Jesus community in Antioch on his own.

"Then Barnabas went to Tarsus to look for Saul, and when he found him, he brought him to Antioch. For a whole year Barnabas and Saul met with the church and taught great numbers of people. The disciples were called Christians first at Antioch." (Acts 11:25-26)

Look at these verses closely:

"...went to Tarsus to *look for* Saul, and when he *found him*, he *brought him* to Antioch."

This sounds easy when read quickly, but this represents a round trip of approximately 400km and (depending on how fast they moved), it would have taken them at least two to three weeks to complete. Imagine how Saul felt when Barnabas knocked on his door. Barnabas *looked* for Saul, eventually *found* him and then *brought* him back to Antioch. When he knocked on Saul's door that day he was not only saying, "I need you", but "I believe in you".

"So for a whole year Barnabas and Saul met with the church and taught great numbers of people." (Acts 11:26)

Today we know Paul as a great teacher and contributor to our understanding of faith in Jesus through his twelve letters, which are now part of our Bible. But back then it was Saul *who*? It was Barnabas who took a chance on Saul, the zealous but untested teacher. It was Barnabas who believed his story and affirmed his call. It was Barnabas who offered Saul his first recorded ministry opportunity. When everyone had forgotten Saul, Barnabas remembered him and helped guide his world-changing ministry to the light.

"Barnabas, on behalf of every follower of Jesus, I thank you."

Can you see the pattern? If we jump into the John Mark story without understanding what happened before, we could conclude that Barnabas' determined behaviour and split with Paul was simply down to blood allegiance and family loyalty. But this would be doing a terrible disservice to Barnabas. His determination to give John Mark a second chance is echoed in his behaviour at Antioch, in his defence and development of Saul, and the reason he was given the name Barnabas in first place.

It is interesting that in the New Testament we have clear examples of every one of the Ephesians 4:11 ascension or ministry gifts. We can see Apostles, Prophets, Teachers and an Evangelist named and at work, but when it comes to Pastor no one is named explicitly. However, if I were designing an Ephesians 4:11 job description for Pastor, my New Testament template (apart from Jesus of course), would be Barnabas. Though named an Apostle (Acts 14:14), he is also the clearest example of what a true Pastor/Shepherd looks like. My granny used to say, "If it looks like a duck, walks like a duck and quacks like a duck… it's probably a duck." For me, Barnabas looked like a Pastor, walked like a Pastor and behaved like a Pastor. The pattern of Acts shows us that his behaviour is not a one-off, but he does what he is, he behaves what he believes, and he offered John Mark a second chance because that is what Pastors do.

When we offer a second chance to the John Marks of our world, what message does it convey to them?

When Barnabas took John Mark, he not only offered redemption from his failure and perceived unfitness, he opened a door to healing, recovery and restoration. In taking him, I believe his actions crystallised and demonstrated three glorious truths that every John Mark needs and wants to hear.

I see and understand you

The Gospel of John tells us that Jesus came full of "grace and truth", and that although the Law came through Moses, "grace and truth" came through Jesus Christ.[3] Grace and truth sit together in constant tension in the ministry of Jesus, for in grace we have the offer of the "Lord's undeserved favour", while in truth we see "reality as the Lord defines it".

3. John 1:14 and 17

These two ideas are on a collision course unless they can be wisely and skilfully managed.

There are many examples of Jesus holding the grace and truth tension within the Gospel of John, but one of my favourites is in John 8:1-11 in the story of the woman "caught in the act of adultery". When she was presented to Jesus in the temple there seemed no way out for the guilty woman; after all she had been "caught" (I wonder how they did that?) Truth, according to Moses, said that she should die (along with the man with whom she committed adultery ... where was he by the way?) During this encounter, Jesus never once refuted this truth, careful not to contradict Moses especially in the temple, but rather He offered grace.

"If any one of you is without sin, let him be the first to throw a stone at her." (v7)

In the absence of a specific accuser, Jesus invited someone in the group to step up – anyone who felt worthy and righteous enough to begin the stoning process. This was a risky strategy indeed, for there may well have been a self-righteous zealot in the crowd who was willing to pick up a stone. But no one did. Thus, without in any way contradicting truth, Jesus appealed to grace. He was not minimising the seriousness of the woman's actions but He was challenging the only option being offered to solve her sinful behaviour. Note how Jesus concluded the story after all her accusers had left the scene:

"Then neither do I condemn you (grace)... go now and leave your life of sin (truth)." (v11)

Jesus won the person and the argument without condoning the sin or abandoning the truth. As a result, the woman received a much needed second chance.

For the follower of Jesus, grace and truth abide as a tension to be managed, not only in how we present the message of Jesus to those who do not yet believe, but in how we appropriate our behaviour to those already within the community of faith. The management of this tension is never easy, demanding both a sensitivity and compassion for the context, while maintaining security and clarity in our convictions. Grace wants to win the person, while truth is determined to win the argument. But without wisdom's guidance it is possible to lose both.

As we listen to Paul and Barnabas argue over John Mark, we hear the clash of grace and truth. Paul led with the truth: *John Mark deserted them.* However, his truth-based conclusion was that he was unfit to carry on. Barnabas argued from grace: *John Mark deserted them.* However, his grace-based conclusion was that his failure was not terminal and he should be given a second chance. Ironically, both men were right, and how we see the world will determine whether we side with Paul's conclusion or Barnabas'. Hindsight offers us perfect vision, but these men had to make a decision in the moment, based on what they knew, what they believed, and what they saw. Paul saw John Mark as he had been, while Barnabas saw what he could become. Truth said, "cut him loose" while grace said "cut him slack". Barnabas could not refute the facts of the case (truth) but he questioned that rejection was the only option on the table (grace).

Facts are facts, and on facts alone there is little room to manoeuvre because it is what it is. However, behind every fact are factors and circumstances, that in themselves do not change the facts but may alter how we understand and respond to them. Without ignoring the truth and the facts about John Mark, Barnabas understood that people don't run without reason and that behind every moment of failure there are complexities worthy of consideration. When truth settles for *what happened*, grace probes for *why it happened*, and in such a search second chances are more likely to be found.

I forgive and accept you

Without forgiveness a second chance is impossible, but even with forgiveness a second chance is not a foregone conclusion. Within the text there are no explicit references to either Paul or Barnabas extending forgiveness to John Mark, but the fact that John Mark was in Antioch, having travelled with them from Jerusalem, suggests that the issue had at least been addressed. It is hard to imagine Paul being comfortable with John Mark making such a journey without a serious conversation having first taken place.

The idea that Barnabas forgave John Mark is easy to accept within the narrative because we know *he took* John Mark with him, but some may struggle to believe that Paul had forgiven John Mark in the light of his rejection. Herein lies another great tension on the journey of faith: forgiveness and reconciliation. Though often framed together, they are in fact two very different decisions and processes. In forgiveness we "cancel a debt" owed to us or "send away an offence" given to us, whereas reconciliation is the "re-joining of two previously separated parties", where two become one again. The clash between Paul and Barnabas over John Mark illustrates this tension perfectly and shows us it is possible to forgive but not accept. Here are four reflections for consideration.

1: Forgiveness is unconditional whereas reconciliation is conditional
Forgiveness requires no condition other than willingness. Reconciliation cannot be processed without certain conditions being addressed and met. Thus, Paul could have forgiven John Mark but refused reconciliation on a personal or ministry level, because conditions important to him had not been met.

2: Forgiveness is personal whereas reconciliation is relational
Forgiveness is something an individual can do on their own and requires no input from the offender whatsoever. Reconciliation is clearly relational and demands a transaction between parties, not just the action of one. Thus, even if Paul had forgiven John Mark, for one reason or another he may not have wanted a continued relationship with the young man, even if John Mark wanted one with him.

3: Forgiveness is focused on release whereas reconciliation is focused on restoration

Forgiveness releases the offended party from both the offence and the offender, breaking the chains that hold the two in a destructive union. Reconciliation is focused on restoring a union fractured by the offence, ensuring that those who walked apart can walk together again. Paul may have understood clearly the need to forgive and be free, but could have been less enthusiastic about restoring his relationship with John Mark, on either a personal or ministry level. It is completely possible that Paul wanted to be free, but not friends!

4: Forgiveness can live without reconciliation whereas reconciliation is impossible without forgiveness

As we try to make sense of Paul's "sharp disagreement" (*paroxusmós*) with Barnabas over John Mark, an understanding of the difference between forgiveness and reconciliation may help explain how both men disagreed, separated and yet carried on in the work of mission. Look at the language from the story:

"Barnabas took Mark and sailed for Cyprus, but Paul chose Silas and left, commended by the believers to the grace of the Lord." (Acts 15:39-40)

Did you catch that? "...commended by the believers to the grace of the Lord". How could such behaviour be commended? Could it be that Paul had forgiven John Mark and that this was clear to all, but he was also open and honest about his struggle to reconcile to a young man he still did not trust? Could it be that the believers in Antioch concluded and accepted that Paul had forgiven John Mark, even though he did not want to work with him? If so, then Paul demonstrates that forgiveness can function without reconciliation.

Clearly Barnabas had no such issues. He was able to progress from forgiveness to reconciliation, enabling him to take John Mark with him.

Paul struggled to accept John Mark, even though I am convinced he forgave him, but it was through acceptance that Barnabas was able to offer John Mark a second chance. Both men did what was essential to ensure they could move forward in freedom, but only Barnabas did what was necessary to ensure that John Mark flourished.

I believe and invest in you

"Barnabas took Mark..."

The word translated "took" here is *paralambáno̅* and the nuance of its meaning is more than just "taking with". Rather, it is "taking near, taking to oneself, or to receive to oneself". I love this idea and the image that Barnabas did not just take John Mark with him to Cyprus, but he took his cousin *to him*, so that John Mark could be *near him*. Could there be a better person to be near than Barnabas the Pastor, the man who liquidated his own property to feed the poor, the man who defended and helped to develop Paul? With a sense of rejection and the word "unfit" echoing in his head, John Mark could not have been near a better person.

Just as Barnabas had believed in Saul enough to look for, find, and bring him back to Antioch, he demonstrated his belief in John Mark by taking hold of him, fighting for him and investing in him. The second chance he extended to Saul while in Tarsus is now offered to John Mark in Antioch, in the hope that the potential he saw in his relative would one day be fully realised.

On arriving in Cyprus, Barnabas and John Mark disappear as players in the narrative of the book of Acts, but no doubt in the silence, the ordinary, the routine and unnoticed moments of life, Barnabas invested, discipled, encouraged and trained John Mark, enabling him to grow as a follower of Jesus, a servant of the Church and an influencer of the good news. Soon, the cousin of Barnabas would become known as "a son" of Peter, but only because he was taken. When Paul wanted to leave him, Barnabas took him, determined to release the untapped ability that lay within, to empower the man the Lord had designed him to be. This second chance was not cheap, easy or superficial, but Barnabas was invested for as long as it took to see the real John Mark emerge.

* * *

As he went down under the water for the fifth time, the young man had reconciled himself to the fact that he was about to drown. Though he couldn't swim, he had ventured from the safety of the beach into the sea near a little Italian town called Paestum. Sinking for what he thought was his final time, he recalls thinking two thoughts: "What a way to begin a honeymoon" and "What is the Italian for 'Help'?" Fortunately, someone saw him struggling in the water and rescued him, depositing him almost unconscious at the feet of his wife. That young, half-dead man, gasping for air was called Jonathan Sacks. In the following years, he would become the Chief Rabbi of the United Hebrew Congregations of the Commonwealth, author of over thirty books, take his place in the House of Lords, and be one of the most respected and influential voices representing biblical thinking in the midst of secular humanist rationale. Though, sadly, he passed away in 2020, he still speaks to me as many of his books adorn my library, and although our views on Jesus differ, he remains my most beloved Jewish author of modern times. Ironically, he never got the name of the person who saved his life, but of the experience he wrote:

"That for me has always been what help is like. You put out a hand, and someone seizes it and lifts you to safety. Self-help would not have worked at all. I was the problem, not the solution. Help, for me, has always been other-help."[4]

Barnabas *put out a hand* and John Mark *seized it.* Through the belief, influence and investment of this wonderful man, John Mark was lifted

4. Jonathan Sacks, *Morality, Restoring the Common Good in Divided Times*, Hodder & Stoughton, UK, 2020, pp.38-39.

to safety and to a life of opportunity and possibility. Barnabas became the other-help for John Mark and by taking him, he dragged him out of the water, prevented him from drowning and became a contributing factor to his success.

Thank God for Barnabas. This selfless man gave himself to Paul and John Mark, enabling both men to go further than he could go himself. He believed in them, invested in them, served them, and became a key component in their success. Ironically, when defending John Mark, Barnabas had to contend *with* his friend Paul in the same way he had once contended *for* him. The risk he took in standing up for Paul to the believers in Jerusalem had paid off. Then, for John Mark, he risked his reputation within the Church and his relationship with Paul, in the hope that his belief and investment would once again pay off.

In affording a second chance to John Mark Barnabas declared, "I see and understand you ... I forgive and accept you... and, I believe and invest in you."

Perhaps you have had a John Mark moment when you were going under and someone reached out a hand and afforded you a second chance.

Do you remember them?

Do you thank the Lord for them?

Have you thanked them?

Do you (if it's possible) bless them?

When we're flying high and all is well, it's easy to forget the Barnabas who pulled us out of the water, challenged us in our stupidity, loved us in our insecurity and stuck with us in our brokenness. To forget such a person is to ignore the *other-help* and deceive ourselves into thinking we made it on our own. Humility never forgets!

Perhaps you have been a Barnabas to a John Mark. Yours was the hand that reached down and pulled up a drowning soul. Maybe they have gone on to greater and better things, and the life-changing role you played has, in some ways, been forgotten. Remember, their success is your success. Their reward will be in part your reward. What people forget the Lord remembers, and the unwritten chapter in their book will always be a part of yours. I love how the writer to the Hebrews put it:

"God is not unjust; He will not forget your work and the love you have shown Him as you have helped His people and continue to help them." (Hebrews 6:10)

Whether remembered and celebrated or not, thank you for being that Barnabas, thank you for reaching out your hand, thank you for being the *other-help* they needed and, for the sake of all John Marks still out there, please never stop!

This morning in my every day devotional reading of the Bible I read a portion from the Gospel of Mark. Though the focus of the passage was on Jesus, which inspired moments of awe and worship in the stillness of my home, I couldn't help but think of the man who jumped into the water and saved the author from drowning. Though Mark wrote the words, through the offer of a second chance, Barnabas made them possible!

"Barnabas, on behalf of every follower of Jesus, I thank you."

Time for Reflection

Paul *rejected* John Mark but Barnabas *took* him. What does this tell us about the personality, purpose and perspective of both men?

"Without forgiveness a second chance is impossible." Though there is no explicit reference to forgiveness in the text, how might we discern the reality of forgiveness through the actions of Barnabas? Why is forgiveness so vital for those offering and benefiting from a second chance?

As you reflect on your own journey, who has been a Barnabas to you? If you've been impacted by a Barnabas:

- Thank God for them and pray for them
- Thank them personally if that is still possible
- Honour and bless them if you can

Perhaps you have been a Barnabas to someone and your role was never fully appreciated. Thank God for them and the privilege you had in serving them. Remember that the Lord sees, He is not unjust, He does not forget, and He will reward you.

6. From Servant to Son

"She who is in Babylon, chosen together with you, sends you her greetings, and so does my son Mark."
(1 Peter 5:13)

If there was anyone who could understand the pain of John Mark's failure and the demands hidden within the process to recovery, it was Peter. Having deserted the Lord in His greatest moment of need and denied Him before sceptical, antagonistic onlookers, Peter understood the depths of despair that failure yields. Of all the people Peter knew, discipled, influenced, supported and trained, John Mark was the only one he called "my son". Even Paul only referred to three people as his sons, namely Timothy (1 Timothy 1:2), Titus (Titus 1:4) and Onesimus (Philemon 10). Men like Luke and Silas were not included in that illustrious category.[1] To be called a son was not some glib generic reference to people connected through faith, rather it reflected a deep, intimate and exclusive relationship. Clearly, a special bond developed between Peter and John Mark, and somewhere in his journey, John Mark moved from the pastoral care of his cousin to the fatherhood of the apostle.

Ironically, it was Mark who was the first one to tell Peter's story of failure to the world, with the other Gospel writers taking their lead from him, adding or omitting details of *his* story as best served their purpose. As we follow Mark, we remind ourselves that his account was influenced by his "father", Peter, so it is striking that in regard to Peter's own fall, a number of key factors recorded in Mark chapter 14 stand out as worthy of note.

1. Dr Luke is referred to as "the beloved doctor" in Col.4:14, the one "with Paul" in 2 Tim.4:11 and "fellow worker" in Philemon 24, but never as a son.

Peter's promise

The day before His death, Jesus had tried to prepare His young followers, telling them that they would "all fall away" from Him. Peter, however, was adamant that,

"Even if all fall away, I will not."

Not for the first time, Jesus pushed back on Peter's push back and dropped the bombshell that Peter would in fact deny Him three times. In classic Peter style, his response to this idea was emphatic:

"Even if I have to die with You, I will never disown You." (v27-31)

Peter was both sincere and determined in his promise to Jesus and, as far as he was concerned, there were no circumstances that would cause him to deny or desert his teacher, Lord and friend. It is the inclusion of this promise in the text that throws a greater spotlight on his eventual denial, yet Peter let Mark include it. I wonder why?

Peter's fatigue

Jesus took all His disciples to Gethsemane for support, but only Peter, James and John were invited to journey further with Him. After a first round of prayer, Jesus returned to the three and found them sleeping:

"'Simon,' He said to Peter, 'are you asleep? Could you not keep watch for one hour?'" (v37)

Did you catch that?

"*Simon*… are *you* asleep?"

James and John were both asleep but only Peter was mentioned. Again, the spotlight falls on his behaviour at that moment. This was a part of the story he could so easily have asked Mark to massage out of the text, but instead it remained part of the final edit. I wonder why?

Peter's response

"Then one of those standing near drew his sword and struck the servant of the high priest, cutting off his ear." (v47)

One of the things I love about the Bible is that it gives us the story warts and all. If you wanted to present a good image of the founding apostles of the Church for future generations, these are the sort of stories that might be on the wrong side of the final cut. However, although Mark included it, he kept the identity of the sword wielding disciple secret and we only know for certain that it was Peter because John revealed his identity (thanks for that John!)[2]

We should remind ourselves that when Peter pulled out his sword that night, he wasn't trying to cut off Malchus' ear (John named him also), he was trying to cut off his head. Peter wanted his life, not his ear! By the time Mark wrote his gospel, Peter's position and reputation as a shepherd, teacher, leader and all round top man was well established in the Church and yet, though Mark may have won the day in keeping Peter's name out of the story, Peter's attempt at murdering someone was recorded. I wonder why?

Peter's desertion

"Then everyone deserted Him and fled." (v30)

Remember Peter's earlier words:

"Even if all fall away, I will not."

Peter leaves his post, abandons his promise and runs, just like the rest of them. Driven by fear he disappeared into the night, although we later learn that he "...followed Him at a distance right into the courtyard of the high priest" (v54).

As alluded to previously, some have suggested that the "young man" who also ran that night was in fact John Mark (a thin but delicious theory). If so, one can only imagine the turmoil within his heart as he penned these words. Whether present or not, it would have been so easy for him to write the story in such a way that, although everyone deserted Jesus and fled, this did not include Peter because he "followed

2. John 18:10

at a distance." I can hear Peter reminding his young scribe, "Let the record reflect that we *all* fled that night, my son." Peter wanted the world to know he was a deserter. I wonder why?

Peter's denial

"He began to call down curses on himself, and he swore to them, 'I don't know this man you're talking about.'" (v71)

Reading this from a 21st century perspective, it is important we don't interpret this as Peter using really bad language – it's much worse than that. When he *swore,* he used the language of oath taking, where someone called on someone or something sacred to guarantee what they said to be true. On top of that, such curses invoked wrath and punishment upon the speaker if what they said turned out to be false! So, if we put this together, Peter asked God to be the guarantor of his words and the judge of his ways. This was much more than a simple denial; this was an aggressive attack on any claim that he was a follower of Jesus. Peter's language could not have been stronger, and it could not have been worse!

How easy it would have been for Mark to simply include the fact that Peter denied Jesus as predicted, but instead he included his "father's" dark, shameful language. I wonder why?

Peter's pain

"And he broke down and wept." (v72)

When the cock crowed, Peter remembered the words Jesus had spoken to him and he broke down. In the face of the crowd in the garden, Peter had been resilient; while surrounded by the antagonism of the courtyard, he had been aggressive; but now, with the words of his friend and teacher echoing in his head he crumbled, unable to maintain his pretence.

Peter was undone. The very things he promised never to do, he had done. Everyone would run but he would not, and all would disown Jesus, but he would not. Now alone and ashamed he wept; a deserter, a denier and a failure. Those of us who have wept such bitter tears look on in humble silence at a man broken by the consequences of his own decisions and overwhelmed by his own shortcomings. Is Peter weeping again as he shares the story with his "son"? Is John Mark weeping as he writes down the story of his "father"? Mark could have moved straight to the moment of Peter's recovery and restoration and skipped the tears, but instead he paused to dwell on Peter's pain and encourages us to do the same. I wonder why?

Peter's second chance

"But go, tell His disciples and Peter." (Mark 16:7)

Don't you love that little addition "and Peter"? It's only found in Mark's account, undoubtedly because it is the bit Peter in particular would have remembered. When the women came back and reported the message, the "and Peter" would have lifted his spirits and his head. All the disciples had fled, but Peter had gone one step further by violently denying Jesus – thus, the special reference that signalled to him the offer of redemption and restoration. John later helps us with the detail of this when he alone includes the story of Jesus and Peter at breakfast. Three times Jesus asked Peter if he loved Him and three times Peter answered that he did. Over breakfast on the beach, Peter got a second chance and history tells us that he seized it with both hands.[3]

Before we move on, one final little thought to consider. In Mark's record of the resurrection, the angel who speaks to the women is described as,

"...a young man dressed in a white robe." (Mark 16:5).

Compare this to an earlier reference from the Gethsemane story:

3. John 21... read the whole glorious chapter

"A young man, wearing nothing but a linen garment, was following Jesus. When they seized him, he fled naked, leaving his garment behind." (Mark 14:51-52)

The phrase "young man" is *neaniskos* and these are the only two times the word is used in this form in the whole of Mark's account. Interestingly, reference is also made to what both young men were wearing, namely a linen cloth (*sindṓn*) and a stately robe (*stolḗ*). If (and it's a big if), the young man in chapter 14 was Mark, then was the description of the angel an allusion to his own failure and restoration, just as the inclusion of "and Peter" was for his "father"?

Peter knew what it was to fall and rise again, and this may be why he took such a keen interest in the young man Paul rejected. Though Peter's story is unique and carries its own facts and nuances, it is also John Mark's story. When Peter saw John Mark favoured by Barnabas and Saul, did it remind him of his own call to follow Jesus and the favour he enjoyed? When Peter heard that John Mark had gone home, did it remind him of his own moment of desertion when he failed in his promise to his Lord? When Peter learned that Paul had rejected John Mark, did it remind Peter of the day over breakfast with Jesus, when he deserved to be rejected but instead was restored and repurposed? John Mark had fallen, but Peter knew from his own experience that the love of a father would ensure he would rise again! Peter determined to be that father.

Peter the father

There is no biblical record that Peter had children of his own. When Jesus healed his mother-in-law, we learned that Peter was married (at that time, the only one of the core twelve), but precious little is told to us about his family. John Mark's father is never mentioned in the text, and it's striking that when Peter is miraculously released from prison, he goes to "...the house of Mary the mother of John, also called Mark..."[4] This might point to the fact that his father had either left the family home or died. The scant details surrounding the families of both men only adds weight to a relationship between a man who had no sons and a son who had no father. Peter became the father John Mark needed and, perhaps, John Mark was the son Peter always wanted!

Having helped raise three children of my own and, through ministry partnerships, tried to raise "sons and daughters" in followership of Jesus, I've discovered that parenting is relentless in its privilege, opportunity and challenge. There have been days when I thought I was doing okay as a dad and other days when I struggled to spell the word dad. I've been blessed with seasons of glory and delight as well as moments of pain and sorrow. However, to see our seed (whether physical or spiritual) grow from infancy to maturity, from potential to reality, and from dependency to interdependency, represents one of the greatest joys imaginable for any parent. I do not feel equipped to offer parenting advice to anyone, and there are many great models and books out there to help us all do it better, but in my journey as a father of my three children and a shepherd of the Lord's children, I have come to understand my responsibility to my *sons and daughters* through three key ideas.

Permission to Know

One of the greatest temptations for any parent is to make their children in their own image. This is totally understandable. We want the best for our kids by helping them to avoid the mistakes we made and by taking advantage of the opportunities we missed or never had. However, our children are not "mini-me's" – they stand in their own right as humans shaped in the image of God, with a unique personhood and purpose. As parents, we are called to model a godly example and create a framework of safety and security. To impose on our children an alien identity, even

4. Acts 12:12. Some believe John Mark's father was called Aristopolis.

if we think it a good one, will not empower them to become or flourish.

John Mark was not Paul, Barnabas, Timothy or Silas. John Mark was John Mark! Peter the father had to resist the temptation to make John Mark a poor imitation of Peter the man and apostle. Even brilliant copies are no match for originals. As a father, Peter had to start with who John Mark was and enable him to become the best version of himself.

Do we hear the echo of this in the life of Jesus? When He stood in the Jordan River, about to be baptised in water; about to be filled with the Spirit and begin His world changing ministry, He heard these words:

"You are My Son, whom I love; with You I am well pleased." (Luke 3:22)

"You are My Son..."

Though "very God of very God", Jesus stood before the world and was acknowledged by His Father as a unique person and representation of God Himself. The writer to the Hebrews proclaimed,

"The Son is the radiance of God's glory and the exact representation of His being, sustaining all things by His powerful word..." (Hebrews 1:3)

Look closely and behold the mystery. Jesus is the "exact representation" yet sustains everything by His "powerful word". Though the Son and Father are one in essence, they are distinct in personhood, and at His baptism this understanding of sameness and difference is celebrated.

If you are a "Peter" to someone today, have the courage to start with who they are and not who you would like them to be. Acknowledge and celebrate the uniqueness of the "John Mark" in your care and perhaps you may have the joy of seeing them become much more than you dared to dream for.

Place to Grow

As well as attempting to father others, I have been enriched by fathers and mothers whose love and investment in me created a place where I could grow. Aside from my own wonderful father and mother, for whom I am eternally grateful, I think of my uncle John, who saw something in a fourteen-year-old boy and gave him his first preaching opportunity. I think of Dr David Petts, the former Principal of Mattersey Hall Bible College, who at my interview realised I would be six weeks short of my eighteenth birthday if I was accepted on the course, but saw something in me and said yes anyway. (I think I hold the record of being the youngest ever Mattersey student).

I'm reminded of John Morgan, who took a risk on an untried, untested and very raw twenty-year-old man fresh out of Bible College, and gave me an opportunity to enter ministry and get paid for the privilege. I often say that John gave me enough rope to fly with, but not enough to hang myself! I recall Colin Hurt, who inspired me with a love for mission. Paul Newberry, who demonstrated that tears while teaching the Word was a great combination. William Williams, the first man I met who taught the Bible like he wrote it, and who threatened to "kick my butt" if I ever messed up. Paul Weaver who courageously invited me onto the National Leadership Team of Assemblies of God (truly I was a boy amongst men) and Ray Belfield who granted me an opportunity to serve with him on his Asia Pacific mission team and opened to me a world beyond my own.

I am so grateful for Professor William Kay, who graciously, generously and lovingly supervised a "bear of very little brain" through my PhD. Throughout my ministry years, I have had one man who has remained a constant influence as both a father and now a friend, and that is David Shearman. So many times, I listened to his wisdom and saw his passion as his tears dripped into his soup over lunch, or onto the Bible as he taught. I have been inspired by his example, encouraged by his investment, rebuked by his challenge and enriched by his love. One of his favourite quotes has also become mine:

"Small boys learn to be large men in the presence of large men who care about small boys."

Each of these people, in their own way, saw something in me and created a place where I could grow. I am a larger man because of their love and investment. I am deeply grateful to them all and to everyone who has contributed to my journey, whether they be named or unnamed.

The problem with growth is that it usually takes time. All my children cooked for nine months in their mother's womb and took a lifetime to raise. In a world obsessed with speed and instant returns, parenting signs up for the long haul with no guarantees that our investment will pay off. Peter signed up for such a journey with John Mark. To bring someone to full recovery after failure and a fall would take time, calling for patience, perseverance, courage and hope. Anyone can invest in a winner – after all, the world loves a winner – but to invest in a fatherless failure and create for them a place of growth, is a call that every parent recognises. Peter created the rich soil in which his son John Mark could grow.

Do we hear the echo of this in the life of Jesus? When He stood in the Jordan River, about to be baptised in water; about to be filled with the Spirit and begin His world changing ministry, He heard these words:

"You are My Son, whom I love; with You I am well pleased." (Luke 3:22)

"...whom I love..."

Jesus went to His world knowing He was loved by His Father. In the silent years, this love had sustained Him, held Him, equipped Him and empowered Him. We can fall into the trap of thinking that Jesus simply did what He did and mechanically fulfilled the mandate of the Father by dying on the cross. But these words point to a deeper motivation and an investment of intimacy, out of which obedience flowed and purpose was formed. The love of the Father to His Son was a place of growth from which Jesus flourished.

If you are *Peter* to someone, one of the greatest gifts you can give them is a place of growth, where the soil is fertilised with belief in them and the environment is saturated with love for them. None of this is a guarantee that they will become all that they should, or that as parents you will be happy with the outcome, but our responsibility is to create the place of growth – it's their responsibility to grow. We can only do what we can do, in the hope that our *sons and daughters* become all they can become.

Power to Go

When my father, Alexander Andrews, left school at fourteen, it was made clear to him that he would amount to very little. These were the final words his old headmaster spoke over him:

"Andrews, I pity you, and I pity the children that come from you."

Though those words neither defined nor crippled my father, they remained in the back of his mind all his life. He married Ruth, the love of his life, and together they raised three children, all of whom loved and served Jesus. When I was a boy, my father took me down to his place of work at the shipbuilders Harland and Wolf, famous for building the Titanic. As a small boy, this was a vast and spacious place, and I saw the world in which my father spent his working days to help provide for his family. He took me to the huge furnaces he helped to clean out for a few extra pounds per week. It was here, as we stood together looking at those furnaces, surrounded by the unforgiving world of the shipyard, that my father said the words I shall never forget:

"Son, I am working down here so you don't have to."

If you knew my father, you would know that this was not a statement of arrogance or a lack of gratitude, rather this was the heart of a father beating with the desire of wanting the best for his children; doing everything he could to ensure they could go further than he had been able to go. My grandfather, father, uncles, and many wider relatives worked down at the shipyard, but I never did. The sacrifice, service and investment of both my parents created a chance to go in a different direction; a direction that my father himself would have loved to have taken.

Posterity has at its heart the meaning of "following" and of investing into a future that is bigger than us. Short-sightedness is the antithesis of parental care, for in our *sons and daughters* we have the embodiment that life will go on after us. The wise person "stores up an inheritance for their children's children", thus creating legacy through the generosity of what has been invested on their behalf. Peter may not have had children of his own, but by investing in John Mark and empowering him to go and become, he not only passed on an inheritance to his *son*, he helped create a legacy *through* his son. Whatever John Mark achieved, it was in no small part due to the fact that Peter empowered him to go.

Do we hear the echo of this in the life of Jesus? When He stood in the Jordan River, about to be baptised in water; about to be filled with the Spirit and begin His world changing ministry, He heard these words:

"You are My Son, whom I love; with You I am well pleased." (Luke 3:22)

"... *with You I am well pleased.*"

These were the words of release. The Father was so delighted in the Son and what He had become (in His human growth), that His pleasure became the launch pad for the Son to move from the obscurity and solitude of the silent years to a public ministry that would culminate in the salvation of the whole world. The Father released the Son to go and do what had never been done before.

If you are a *Peter* to a *John Mark,* your ultimate goal is their release, their sending and their going. As parents we might want to keep them close, and if that is part of their "going", then that's okay. But one of the worst things we can do for them is to keep them close when they should go, or hold onto them when they should be released.

Peter became a father to John Mark, no doubt drawn by the brokenness of where the young man had come from, while driven by the prospect of where he could go and who he could become. Peter reached out to the fatherless failure and raised John Mark as *his son*, giving him permission to know, a place to grow and the power to go!

"... my son John Mark."

Time for Reflection

Peter knew what it was to fall and rise and he knew the pain of failure and the joy of restoration. What principles of truth and practices of faith can transform our pain into a platform of healing and service to others?

Good "fathers" (I use *father* in the context of this chapter but generically it includes all *parents*) give *permission to know*. When nurturing and discipling others, why is it vital to start with "who you are" rather than "I want you to be"?

Good "fathers" create a *place to grow*. Though every *John Mark* is unique, what core ideas must be present to create a place of growth? In what environment do you or have you grown best?

Good "fathers" enable the *power to go*. What attitudes need to reside in us to facilitate the release of others to be greater than us?

7. Make Him Welcome

"My fellow prisoner Aristarchus sends you his greetings, as does Mark, the cousin of Barnabas. (You have received instructions about him; if he comes to you, welcome him)."
(Colossians 4:10)

Over my lifetime I've discovered that most people struggle to admit that they got things wrong. An authentic acknowledgement that we made a bad call or took the wrong direction is rare, let alone addressing the consequences of our mistakes. Paul's letter to the church at Colosse was his first *public* reference to John Mark since his split with Barnabas. Most scholars accept that this letter was written around 62AD, when Paul was in prison in Rome, and if that is the case, then this mention comes approximately 13-14 years after Paul declared John Mark "unfit" for purpose.[1] Yet, in this brief comment towards the end of his letter, Paul seems to admit that his conclusion about John Mark was proved wrong and he now seeks a way to heal the hurt he caused and put right his mistake:

"You have received *instructions about him*; if he comes to you, *welcome him*."

At the same time as Paul wrote this letter to the believers in Colosse, he wrote another letter to his friend Philemon who, coincidently, also lived in Colosse. In fact, according to Paul's letter to him, we discover that the church there met in his home, suggesting that Philemon was not only a man of sincere love who gave Paul "great joy and encouragement", and of generous faith that "refreshed the hearts of the saints", but he was also a man of significant wealth.[2]

---

1. N.T. Wright suggests that both the letters to Colossians, Ephesians and Philemon may have been written as early as 55-56AD, from his imprisonment in Ephesus. *Paul, A Biography*, SPCK, UK, 2018, pp.433-434
2. Verse 7

Although the letter to the church is for everyone, the letter to Philemon is deeply personal (I'm so glad it was made public for our benefit), as Paul sought to address a painful and potentially fractious issue with one of his dearest friends. One of Philemon's slaves, a young man called Onesimus, had not only run away from his master, but we suspect had also stolen from him. Remarkably, while on the run, he connected with Paul and became "his son in the faith", so Paul sent him back to repair what he had broken, appealing to Philemon "on the basis of love."[3]

Both letters have some striking similarities. They were written by the same man, at more or less the same time, to believers in the same city, and when we compare Paul's request to the Colossians on behalf of John Mark and those to Philemon on behalf of Onesimus, they carry the same appeal. Just as Paul gave instructions regarding John Mark and urged the believers in Colosse to "welcome him", he does the same in his letter to Philemon, outlining detailed instructions and asking his friend to "welcome him as you would welcome me".[4]

On both counts, Paul's tone of compassion, tenderness and courage is identical, as the "old man in chains" made a way for the young men under his care. Therefore, as we try to understand how Paul attempted to help John Mark, his letter to Philemon on behalf of his son Onesimus might enable us to hear his love between the lines. Before you read any further, why not take a moment to read the twenty-five glorious verses contained in the book we call Philemon.

With the letter to Philemon in your head, now read these words again:

"My fellow prisoner Aristarchus sends you his greetings, as does Mark, the cousin of Barnabas. (You have received instructions about him; if he comes to you, welcome him)." (Colossians 4:10)

---

3. Verse 9
4. Verse 17

When we look at Paul's words regarding John Mark, three things immediately stand out. The first is that John Mark was clearly *with* Paul, hence Paul was able to send his greetings. This is also borne out in Philemon, where Paul concluded,

"Epaphras, my fellow-prisoner in Christ Jesus, sends you greetings. And so do Mark, Aristarchus, Demas and Luke, my fellow-workers." (v23-24)

I'm going to revisit this in detail in the next chapter, but we cannot move on without at least recognising that John Mark was now serving *with* Paul, and it was probably out of this context of service that Paul was able to appeal with confidence on his behalf. Thus, the next two requests from Paul we're about to consider must be heard in the light of a significant shift in the relationship between the two men. Somewhere in the past they became both friends and fellow-workers.

Words of clarity

"You have received instructions about him..."

The word translated "instructions" here is *entolē* and points to an authoritative direction or instruction to do something through writing or speech. This word is used by Jesus when He speaks of the "commands" of the Father in His own life and ministry.[5] Paul, then, was giving a clear directive to the churches in relationship with him about how John Mark was to be treated. We have no idea what those instructions were, but observing the pattern of his instructions regarding Onesimus might give us some idea of what Paul said and why.

Onesimus needed help to return to Philemon and Paul provided that help. (Ironically, I suspect that Paul sounded much like Barnabas did, when he tried to help John Mark return in Acts 15). Paul understood that his instructions could not only enable Onesimus to return, but they might also empower Philemon to receive. Though Paul (less than subtly)

5. John 10:18, 12:49-50

states he could "be bold and order" Philemon to receive Onesimus, he knew that would not work, so he appealed on the basis of three things.

Paul acknowledged what Onesimus did

"If he has done you any wrong or owes you anything, charge it to me." (v18)

Paul explained what Onesimus became

"...who became my son while I was in chains." (v10)

Paul expressed what Onesimus could be

"...but now he has become useful..." (v11)

"I would have liked to keep him with me..." (v12)

"...better than a slave, as a dear brother in the Lord." (v16)

By writing in this way, Paul was placing his own reputation on the line on behalf of Onesimus, to enable the young slave to *rise* after his terrible *fall.* This alone would have carried enormous weight in Philemon's mind, and whatever he thought of his slave, he could not easily dismiss the enormity of Paul's vulnerability.

Was this how Paul instructed the churches regarding John Mark?

Did the fact that Paul himself issued "instructions concerning him", putting his own reputation, position and authority on the line with his endorsement, carry significant weight with the churches?

If Paul's directives regarding John Mark reflect the spirit of what was written to Philemon, then it would have been impossible for the believers at Colosse and beyond to ignore or dismiss such an appeal.

Just as Onesimus needed help to return to Philemon, so John Mark needed help to return to the churches Paul was in special relationship with, and Paul realised that he was the only one who could make that happen. In light of their previous split, there were some things that John

Mark could not do or say on his own behalf; things that Paul alone could do for him. If Paul remained silent, suspicion would forever remain over the reputation and ministry of the "son of Peter". Paul's words not only brought clarity, but granted liberty and opportunity. If John Mark was to *rise* to all the potential that was within him, the *fall* in his past could not be ignored. Where Paul's words about John Mark in the past had blocked his path, now his instructions about John Mark opened a way.

This new way was opened by granting two things for John Mark:

Firstly, *public closure.*

Events grow legs and few stories escape the clutches of rumour, exaggeration, misinformation and bias. I am sure this was as true for the Jesus-centric, Spirit-filled citizens of the first century as it is for ours. Under the pretext of "please pray for...", many a tale has been told, and in defending a position, rumours replace reality, lies shape truth, and misinformation frames an ongoing narrative. In my own journey of public Christian ministry, I've experienced the merciless, relentless challenge of a narrative outside my control, where people have chosen to believe the worst and accepted the (non-biblical maxim), "there's no smoke without fire".

Was this John Mark's position?

If it was, then he was caught in the horns of a dilemma. If he defended himself, it might be seen as an attack on Paul and an expression of his own pain and ego. If he remained silent, it might be interpreted as an admission of guilt.

Was this why Paul sent his instructions?

Paul had within his pen the power of closure. His instructions could squash the rumours, clarify any misinformation, dispel the clouds of doubt and free John Mark from the burden of explanation. Paul's instructions enabled John Mark to return and empowered the churches to receive him.

Secondly, *personal confidence.*

Ambiguity is the breeding ground of insecurity. When a person is unsure of how they are seen and understood, they will invariably be uncertain as to how they will be received. Not everyone has the resolve to live with a question mark attached to their integrity and character, especially over a prolonged period of time. Even on our best days this can be exhausting, and I am convinced that many a *John Mark* has given up, not because their character was weak, but because their confidence was shot!

I love football and sometimes when discussing a footballer's loss of form, a pundit might say, "He's a confidence player, and because his confidence has gone everything else is suffering." But isn't that the same for everyone? All of us are confidence players because all of us, to a lesser or greater extent, need confidence to play.

One word from Paul, the man who had previously deemed him "unfit", had the power to change all this for John Mark. No longer would he have to live with a question mark, now public closure would open the door to renewed personal confidence. If Paul's instructions about John Mark echoed his fierce, passionate defence of Onesimus, then renewed confidence would have flooded into his heart, empowering him to go forward into his future with boldness. Instead of looking over his shoulder or wondering what people thought of him, John Mark could now enter any room that honoured Paul with both security and strength.

Ironically, many years before Barnabas had done exactly the same thing for a very young, zealous Saul:

"But Barnabas took him and brought him to the apostles. He told them how Saul on his journey had seen the Lord and that the Lord had spoken to him, and how in Damascus he had preached fearlessly in the name of Jesus. So Saul stayed with them and moved about freely in Jerusalem, speaking boldly in the name of the Lord." (Acts 9:27-28)

The *instructions* of Barnabas had granted public closure and personal confidence to Saul. Now, years later, Paul does the same for Barnabas' cousin John Mark.

Actions of charity

"...if he comes to you, welcome him."

How we are welcomed may determine whether or not we stay. In the letters Paul wrote to the church at Colosse and his friend Philemon, he asked that two individuals be welcomed.

On behalf of John Mark he wrote:

"...if he comes to you, welcome him."

The word translated "welcome" is *déchomai* and points to the idea of accepting an offer deliberately and readily, thus to take or receive what is presented or brought by another. In this context, Paul is "offering" John Mark to Colosse and, by implication, all the churches who relate specifically to him. He is asking them as a *community* to receive and welcome John Mark.

On behalf of Onesimus he wrote:

"So if you consider me a partner, welcome him as you would welcome me." (v17)

Paul appealed to Philemon on a much more personal basis using the word *koinōnós*, translated "partner" in this verse. Paul and Philemon had a friendship that was neither superficial nor casual, but deep and meaningful. This might explain why Paul used a different word for welcome than that used to Colosse. The word used there is *proslambánō* and leans into the idea not just of receiving but of taking or receiving *to oneself*. Paul is asking Philemon not to simply receive Onesimus back into his house as a slave assigned to his quarters, rather he is asking him to take Onesimus *to himself*!

I heard someone once say that we should go where we are "celebrated not tolerated". Although we must be careful how we understand and appropriate such an idea, over the years this has helped me to come to terms with the fact that not every welcome is the same. Paul asked the church to welcome John Mark (if he comes) and asked Philemon to welcome Onesimus when he was sent back. However, the issue was not only *if* a welcome would be extended, but *how*. Remember, how we are welcomed may determine whether or not we stay.

For those rising from a fall, how a welcome is extended to them is crucial, and over the years I have seen and experienced two types of welcome for *John Marks* (and Onesimus') as they seek to return.

The Welcome of Responsibility

The first is a welcome of duty; a welcome of toleration.

"We are family… therefore you are welcome."

"We are in Christ… therefore you are welcome."

"We are part of the same church… therefore you are welcome."

"We have been asked to welcome you… therefore you are welcome."

Any welcome is better than no welcome, but the welcomes of responsibility, duty and toleration are only marginally better. We have all been in awkward social situations where we were welcomed but somehow didn't feel accepted, and the discomfort of such a feeling generally means exiting the building as early as possible. The welcome of responsibility won't give *John Mark* what he or she needs and if the welcoming community doesn't understand this, then the opportunity for true restoration will be missed. Doing our bit by opening the door is good, but often not enough. Those who are trying to rise after a fall need open hearts and open arms, not just open doors. There is a difference between a generic offer ("You are welcome here any time") and a specific invitation ("We would love you to come for dinner, so let's fix a date.")

The welcome of responsibility is better than rejection, but only just. When responsibility alone determines our welcome, *John Mark* hears "please come in" but experiences "please don't stay", and it permits the welcoming community to open their door without opening their hearts. Under such a welcome the fallen rarely rise.

The Welcome of Redemption

The second is a welcome of joy; a welcome of celebration.

One of the greatest redemptive welcomes in the whole of the gospels is that depicted by Jesus in the parable of the lost sons.[6] A casual reading of this parable is emotionally powerful, but when understood in the context of its original culture, my emotions go into overdrive. It was Kenneth Bailey who first alerted me to the practice of *Kezazah* (the cutting off). The actions of the younger son were culturally disgraceful, as he not only demanded his inheritance but then squandered it. If such a person returned to their home village, *Kezazah* directed that the community would break a large pot in front of him and cry out, "(the name of the person) is cut off from his people." Then he would be obliged to sit outside the gate of his family home in abject humiliation before seeing his father. Eventually his father would summon him and ask him to apologise before sending him (effectively banishing him) to the next village.[7]

Now read the story Jesus told again. The father does the exact opposite to what is expected. He runs to his son before the villagers with pot in hand can get to him, and when he gets to him we hear these glorious words:

"But the father said to his servants, 'Quick! Bring the best robe and put it on him. Put a ring on his finger and sandals on his feet. Bring the fattened calf and kill it. Let's have a feast and celebrate. For this son of mine was dead and is alive again; he was lost and is found.' So they began to celebrate." (Luke 15:22-24)

---

6. Luke 15:11-32. This is often referred to as the story of the Prodigal son, but the parable begins "There was a man who had two sons…" (v 11). Both the context of when and to whom the story is told calls us to read it with two sons in mind.
7. Kenneth E. Bailey, *The Cross and the Prodigal*, IVP, USA, 2005, pp.52-74

I love the literal meaning of the word translated "celebrate". The word is *euphraínō* and can literally read "well mind". The father was not just fulfilling his external duty, rather he was happy and well from the inside out. The external party was a sign of his internal joy. This is not the welcome of responsibility or duty or toleration... this is the welcome of redemption. The son was embraced and celebrated, and through such a welcome was given a genuine opportunity to rise from his fallenness. The welcome of redemption is the welcome of *second chance* and is, of course, dramatically contrasted by the response of the father's eldest son. We learn that he was "angry", "refused to go in", and by implication did not "celebrate".

How is your welcome?

If you've ever been on the wrong side of failure or rejection you'll know that a welcome can either be powerful or destructive. What makes the difference in the journey of any *John Mark* is not if a welcome is extended but how. It is hard to rise from fallenness in a place of toleration, created by a welcome of responsibility. While the welcome of redemption, and the place of celebration it creates, is no guarantee of success, the probability and possibility of authentic recovery and lasting restoration is dramatically increased.

"My fellow prisoner Aristarchus sends you his greetings, as does Mark, the cousin of Barnabas. (You have received instructions about him; if he comes to you, welcome him)."

It is easy to read these words and miss their power. Approximately fourteen years have passed since the infamous split, and in that time both life and people have changed. The rise of John Mark was possible because three men played an important role. Barnabas *took him*, Peter *adopted him* and Paul *endorsed him*. The contribution these three men represent are crucial if those who fall (for whatever reason) are to rise again. John Mark survived because someone continued to believe in him, even in failure. John Mark grew because someone invested in him and nurtured the gift that lay within, becoming the father he needed. John Mark prospered in his ministry and influence because someone accepted him, endorsed him and promoted him.

The recovery of all *John Marks* is neither quick, cheap or easy, but if such love abounds, it remains a glorious redemptive possibility.

Time for Reflection

Take a moment to read Paul's letter to Philemon. In what ways might Paul's defence of Onesimus have been shaped by his experience (past and present) with John Mark?

John Mark needed Paul's help. Why were the words of Paul so important in regard to the reputation and ministry of John Mark?

Someone once said, "Go where you are celebrated not tolerated". What factors can help move toleration to celebration?

For those extending a welcome, what are the differences between the "welcome of responsibility" and the "welcome of redemption"? What might the impact of either welcome have on the recipient?

8. No Greater Compliment

"Only Luke is with me. Get Mark and bring him with you, because he is helpful to me in my ministry."
(2 Timothy 4:11)

Someone once said that "the threat of execution concentrates the mind". The letter from Paul that we call 2 Timothy contains the last recorded words of the great apostle, before he joined the growing number of saints martyred for Jesus. Paul's fight was almost fought, and his race almost finished, but before he put away his quill for good, he gave us one final gloriously tender glimpse into the story of John Mark.

The closing remarks of Paul, captured for us in 2 Timothy 4:9-22, are some of the most personal and vulnerable words he wrote. Imprisoned and facing imminent execution, we feel his pain as he describes the desertion of Demas and the harm caused by Alexander; and that he felt abandoned by everyone during his "first defence". He concludes,

"But the Lord stood at my side and gave me strength." (v17)

As he asks for "the cloak" that he left with "Carpus at Troas", as well as his scrolls and parchments, the sense of urgency is tangible as he pleads with Timothy his "son":

"Do your best to get here before winter..." (v21)

As he concludes his letter, he commends Luke for being with him then proceeds to write one of his most redemptive sentences:

"Get Mark and bring him with you, because he is helpful to me in my ministry." (v11)

In the previous chapter we observed Paul sending instructions to the church on behalf of John Mark, thus making a way for him to freely serve them, while empowering the believers at Colosse and beyond to generously receive him. Now he is sending instructions to John Mark (via Timothy), so that he can come to him personally at his time of greatest need. As we have followed John Mark's journey, from his *fall* to his *rise*, these eleven words in Greek form a high water mark in his relationship with Paul and demonstrate to us the relentless power of a *second chance.*

Let us take a moment to look closer and marvel at these eleven magnificent words that celebrate how far John Mark had come in Paul's estimation.

From rejection to acceptance

"*Get Mark* and *bring him* with you..."

As we read these words, we cannot help but hear the echo of previous words recorded by Luke:

"Barnabas wanted to *take John*, also called Mark, with them, but Paul did not think it wise to *take him*..." (Acts 15:37)

By refusing Barnabas' appeal, Paul rejected John Mark by not taking him on their proposed second missional journey but now, years later, he wants Timothy to bring John Mark to him. The statement could literally read, "...having taken, bring (him) with you..." From the previous chapter we know that Paul had already reconnected with John Mark, even though the biblical text is silent on when, where and how. So, this request (command) is not a shock or a surprise, but one that affirms the growing relationship between the two men. Nevertheless, I cannot help but feel that Paul's specific use of the language of acceptance was deliberate in light of his previous rejection.

Why was this such a powerful compliment from Paul?

This is a compliment to John Mark's *character.*

Having been rejected by Paul, John Mark showed the maturity to return to him and walk with him. As he left for Cyprus that day, he must have felt the sting of rejection and the pain of Paul's words, and this experience would either become a prison house that defined the rest of his life, or an opportunity to listen, learn, grow and change. Somebody once said that "character is what we do when no one is looking", and as John Mark disappeared over the horizon with Barnabas, few may have shown interest in his future. Even the story of Acts makes no further reference of him.

In the unseen world, away from the spotlight of Luke's narrative, John Mark had some character choices to make in the light of Paul's conclusions about him. Somewhere in the silence he came to terms with the darkness and pain of his rejection, for although he disappeared from the story for a while, he returned restored and rejuvenated. Character is built on values and beliefs that are expressed through our behaviour, and so for Paul to ask for John Mark in this way showed that he had seen in the young man's life the development and demonstration of his character. Whatever had caused John Mark to desert his post all those years ago had been identified and addressed. Whatever John Mark felt about Paul's decision to reject him had been brought to the light and released through forgiveness. So, when Paul called for John Mark to come to him, it was an affirmation of John Mark's maturity and proven character.

It is so easy to allow the opinions and actions of others to define who we are and what we become, especially when they come from people we've loved and trusted. Character is not formed by the crucible of rejection, but it is revealed by it. When touched by pain, we discover who we are at that moment and what we truly believe. Our reactions to rejection (if we're honest), are as much about who we are and what we believe, as about what the other party did. Thus, a potential moment of revelation occurs, where through the spotlight of self-awareness, we are given the opportunity to listen, learn, grow and change.

Am I prepared to accept what I now see and hear in *my reaction* that needs to change?

Is there something *in me* that, if un-challenged, may allow this rejection to seed my destruction?

This, of course, is not to minimise in any way what others have said or done, but rather to lead us to higher ground, and with it the opportunity for a second chance.

From unfit to useful

"Get John Mark and bring him to me, because *he is helpful…*"

The word translated "helpful" here is *eúchrēstos*, (from *eú* meaning "well" and *chráomai*, "to furnish what is needful"). It points to the idea of something or someone being useful or profitable. This is in stark contrast to Paul's previous assessment of John Mark, when he deemed him *unfit* for the task before them (Acts 15:38). Paul used *eúchrēstos* three times in his letters and every time he used it of people in both a general and specific sense. Earlier in 2 Timothy he wrote,

"Those who cleanse themselves from the latter will be instruments for special purposes, made holy, *useful* to the Master and prepared to do any good work." (2 Timothy 2:21)

When he wrote to Philemon concerning Onesimus he concluded,

"Formerly he was useless to you, but now he has become *useful* both to you and to me." (Philemon 11)

In the previous chapter we compared the similarities of his letter to Philemon on behalf of Onesimus to that written to the Colossians, containing remarks on behalf of John Mark. Now, in these final words to Timothy concerning John Mark, we see another unmistakable connection to his previous appeal to Philemon on behalf of "his son" Onesimus:

Onesimus: "Formerly he was *useless* (to Philemon)… he has become *useful…*"

John Mark: Previously he was judged *unfit* (by Paul in Acts 15), but now "…he is *helpful/useful/profitable…*"

Why was this such a powerful compliment from Paul?

This is a compliment to John Mark's *competence.*

Though we may not have all the details of what John Mark did with Barnabas, then Peter, we know that he served. No one is declared useful without being useful, and usefulness finds expression through service. There is no way that Paul could have confidently concluded that John Mark was useful unless he had already proven his usefulness to him and others. But his usefulness was not just down to his ability, it included his attitude. John Mark could have allowed revenge to fuel his usefulness, motivated by the desire to prove Paul wrong. But revenge is a terrible taskmaster that is never satisfied and which never grants satisfaction. Had John Mark been driven by revenge, his usefulness would have been contaminated and toxic.

Doing the right thing is good, but doing it for the right reason is best. Serving others is good, but serving from freedom is best. Generosity is good, but generosity with joy is best. The passage of time would test John Mark's motivation. If his usefulness to Barnabas was about showing up Paul, then time itself would turn his enterprise to dust. The silent, unseen years would test the quality of John Mark's competence.

Our usefulness in life is not merely determined by our abilities but also by our attitudes. How we serve (the condition of our hearts) is as important to the Lord as what we do (the contribution of our hands). We must not allow our usefulness to be defined by the superficiality of our actions alone, rather we must have the courage to dig deeper, ensuring our attitudes remain part of our estimation. When our usefulness emerges from the attitudes of our heart, not just the actions of our hands, then we will be useful wherever we are, whoever we are with, and whether our usefulness is acknowledged by others or administered in secret. The slow passage of time tests our attitudes more than our actions, but if our attitudes remain spiritually sound, dynamic service will always follow.

From doubt to trust

"Get John Mark and bring him to me, because he is helpful *to me*..."

I love the personal nature of this affirmation. In Paul's estimation, John Mark wasn't just useful to Barnabas or Peter or Colosse, or even to Jesus, he made it clear that John Mark was useful to *him*! When Paul and Barnabas experienced their painful and fracturing *paroxusmós*, Barnabas took John Mark, whereas, we are told,

"...Paul *chose* Silas..." (Acts 15:40)

Paul *chose* Silas over John Mark. Paul placed his trust in Silas; a trust that was vindicated in the persecution and prison cells of Philippi. Back then, Paul could not and would not trust a young man who had deserted his post, but now, having been abandoned by many in his time of need, his attention turned specifically to John Mark, in confidence that he would come to him. Of all the people he could have chosen, *he chose him*. Of all the people Paul trusted, *he trusted him*.

Why was this such a powerful compliment from Paul?

This is a compliment to John Mark's *consistency*.

Paul now chose John Mark because he could trust him, and his choice was a declaration of that trust. Relational trust does not appear by magic or get deposited when a man or woman of God lays hands on us, rather it is built over time. In the years between John Mark's rejection and his return, time would test the perseverance needed to build trust and probe for the authenticity and transparency it demands. Trust develops slowly but can be destroyed quickly and John Mark had destroyed Paul's trust in him. How could John Mark show himself trustworthy again? The key to building trust would be in the consistency of his character and contribution. If John Mark could show godly character consistently, and if his contribution was consistently useful and profitable, then his trustworthiness would grow and opportunities would follow. The silent, unseen years of John Mark's journey to recovery would brutally test his consistency, but it seems he passed that test with flying colours.

Trustworthiness demands consistency. If we are to convince people in our world to give to us one of the most precious commodities they possess, their trust, then we must, over time, consistently prove ourselves to be worthy of that trust. Trust cannot be demanded or commanded, rather trust is nurtured in soil where there is a consistent commitment to all that is good. Anyone can look good for a moment or be brilliant for a day, but trust from others does not yield so easily to such superficiality, and our trustworthiness will not flourish in shallow soil. Consistency moves the occasional to become normal, infusing routine, everyday moments with power and life. As John Mark had to learn, and Paul through his words affirmed, the passage of time will test not only our character and our competence but our consistent commitment to both. On such, trust is built.

From failure to fellow-worker

"Get John Mark and bring him to me, because he is helpful to me *in my ministry.*"

This is the crowning glory of Paul's words and a phrase that must have been like balm to John Mark's soul. Not only was John Mark useful to Paul personally, but was declared useful to Paul's ministry. The word translated "ministry" is *diakonía* and has at its heart the meaning of service. These words again send us back to Acts 15. We recall that John Mark had been with them "...as their helper", or as their *under-rower* (Acts 13:5), but later Luke tells us that John Mark,

"...had not continued with them in the work." (Acts 15:38)

However, in this final phrase of Paul's final written comment about John Mark, the tone has changed dramatically. Paul no longer sees John Mark as an under-rower, but as someone serving alongside him, as a partner and not a junior. If confirmation were needed that this was in Paul's mind as he wrote, then his earlier words to Philemon provide it:

"Epaphras, my fellow prisoner in Christ Jesus, sends you greetings. And so do Mark, Aristarchus, Demas and Luke, *my fellow workers*." (Philemon 23-24)

Whereas in Acts, Paul may have viewed John Mark as one working *for* him or *under* him, these words heralded John Mark as one of Paul's *sunergói* – one working *with* him!

Why was this such a powerful compliment from Paul?

This is a compliment to John Mark's *capacity.*

To be described as one working *with* Paul implies that, in Paul's estimation, John Mark had the capacity to rise to such a position and fulfil its demands. As we've seen already, Paul believed that John Mark had the ability to be useful, but by inviting him to serve with him in his ministry as a fellow worker, Paul was declaring that John Mark had the capacity to maximise his usefulness. Paul was a hard person to work for/with, having a huge physical, intellectual and spiritual capacity of his own, as evidenced in his travels, writings and purpose. No doubt many loved the idea of joining Paul's team but, for one reason or another, few lasted the pace, as his own reflections hint. In the passage in which John Mark is commended, we are told that Demas *forsook* Paul, Alexander *hurt* Paul and many others (Paul says everyone) *abandoned* him. The old apostle was totally confident that John Mark had the capacity to walk, work, and serve beside and with him. This is high praise indeed for the man who struggled to serve as an *under-rower* all those years before.

All of us have limits to our abilities and capacity and such limits, if properly understood, are not meant to hurt but help us. Limitations and boundaries can be a source of freedom not restriction. However, most of us live well within our limitations, rarely venturing to places where we can grow in character and expand the range of our competencies. From the opening pages of the Scriptures we see the Lord establishing this principle of expansion, asking two people to "rule the earth, subdue the earth and fill the earth", as He encouraged them to take the delight of Eden and replicate it across the globe. For the man and the woman, the issue wasn't competence but capacity. They already had everything they needed but they would have to embrace the challenge of growing into the task. We cannot be what we are not and we cannot do what we are not gifted to do, but our capacity can grow in both areas, so that we become a greater version of our God-shaped self and see our gifts and abilities go further than we ever thought possible.

As I've journeyed with Jesus as a follower, teacher and leader, I've discovered three reoccurring principles that impact my capacity, positively or negatively. These principles are built on a foundation where Jesus is at the centre, where we delight in His Word and where the Holy Spirit is wanted and welcomed.

The convictions I hold

"Above all else guard your heart, for it is the wellspring of life." (Proverbs 4:23)

What truth this proverb holds. It teaches me that the condition of my heart has the power to touch every part of my life and even determine the boundary for it. Nothing on the outside of my world operates without the influence of my heart, and this verse has taught me that my boundaries are not set by what is around me, but by what is within me. Seeing my capacity expand is, in part, dependent on the condition of my heart, and my heart is shaped and fed by the beliefs I accept and hold. Therefore, my convictions feed my heart and my heart determines the quality and extent of the flow of my life.

The company I keep

"He who walks with the wise grows wise, but a companion of fools suffers harm." (Proverbs 13:20)

I've discovered that the company I keep can have a direct impact on the way I think and the things I do, and although this alone is not the determining factor of my capacity, I ignore this at my peril. Being in the company of the wise exposes me to people who may be smarter, bigger and deeper than myself. Being with the wise casts a spotlight on my own comfort and ease and provokes me with the reality that the world is bigger than me, my preferences and my sphere of influence. As we've touched on in a previous chapter, John Mark grew bigger in the presence of big people who loved him and so the capacity of his heart and life enlarged. Our capacity is not solely dependent on the company we keep but it will always be impacted by it.

The challenges I accept

"The wicked man flees though no one pursues, but the righteous are as bold as a lion." (Proverbs 28:1)

I love my routines and the comfort of a world where everything is known and in its place, but I've discovered that as lovely as this is, it can subtly limit my capacity by discouraging me from venturing beyond the borders of my comfort. There is nothing wrong with comfort unless it becomes controlling. Many of my dynamic moments of growth have coincided with my greatest seasons of challenge. The willingness to embrace such challenge stretches me and over the years has shown me that I was able to go further as a person and do more with my abilities than I thought. It is much easier to run from the challenge, but in such moments we shrink a little. However, to embrace the challenge with boldness, whatever the outcome, usually ensures our capacity will increase. In whatever way John Mark grew, something happened in the silent, unseen years that transformed him from an *under-rower* to a *fellow-worker*.

The focus of this chapter has been on John Mark and rightly so. As we have slowly considered the fourfold nature of Paul's compliment, we marvel at his rise after such a dramatic fall. Our hearts are stirred by his story of recovery, restoration and re-purposing, captured in Paul's final words. However, having considered this eleven-word sentence, saturated with hope, joy and redemption, it would be remiss not to reflect on the humility with which this beautiful compliment was written.

Over the years people have asked me, "When it comes to John Mark, who got it right, Barnabas or Paul?" When I answer, "Both", I am normally confronted with frowns of confusion. I truly believe Barnabas was right. Giving John Mark a second chance was the compassionate thing to do, and ultimately proved to be a stroke of genius. But I also believe Paul was right. I get why Paul was so hard on the young man and why he didn't want to risk the success of the mission on someone who might go AWOL again. For Paul, there was no room for sentiment, only a commitment to the cause and, as history shows, that's part of the reason Paul made the impact he did. However, Paul's final words to John Mark, via the hand of his son Timothy, reflect transparent honesty and authentic humility, bringing sensitive closure to a difficult moment for Paul, Barnabas and John Mark. Paul's explicit generosity to John Mark and his implicit honour of his old friend Barnabas speak loudly through his words and between the lines. Paul, about to meet his executioner, does not leave things unsaid that needed to be said. I wonder, did Barnabas get to read or hear his comments? If he did, my imagination permits me only to see Pastor Barnabas receive these words with joy in his heart and tears in his eyes.

"Get Mark and bring him with you, because he is helpful to me in my ministry."

With these words of honour, hope and humility Paul's story is about to come to an end, but for John Mark, more glorious chapters are about to be written.

Time for Reflection

It is one thing for Paul to ask for John Mark, but another thing entirely for him to go. What does it tell us about John Mark's growth in character, that he would return to serve Paul?

"There is no way that Paul could have confidently concluded that John Mark was useful unless he had already proven his usefulness to him and others." Why is remaining *useful* the most noble response in the face of being regarded *unfit*? How can we live usefully without it becoming an act of vengeance?

"Trust cannot be demanded or commanded, rather trust is nurtured in soil where there is a consistent commitment to all that is good." In regaining trust, patience is vital. What are the enemies to the patience needed to build trust? What truths can help encourage and sustain our patience?

Take time to consider the three principles that impact our capacity.

The convictions I hold
Is there something you believe (about the Lord, yourself or your context), that consistently resists the expansion of your capacity?

The company I keep
Are the friends and voices in your world helping you to become what you can be in Christ Jesus or keeping you small?

The challenges I accept
Some challenges are as much about what is achieved in us as what is accomplished through us. If we viewed challenge through the lens of personal growth and not just as an opportunity, how might this change our approach to the challenge?

9. Stump-fingered Storyteller

"Between my finger and my thumb the squat pen rest. I'll dig with it."
(Seamus Heaney)

The opening statement of the Bible is conveyed to us in seven Hebrew words. It speaks confidently from its wholeness and perfection, confronting the reader/listener with truth that is both dramatic and emphatic. Hundreds of years after Moses penned those words, Mark began his account of the life of Jesus using seven Greek words, and with no less confidence and drama he declared,

"The beginning of the gospel of Jesus Christ, Son of God." (Mark 1:1)[1]

In Moses' beginning, we are introduced to Elohim, the author of creation and to the One who brought the world and humanity into being. In Mark's beginning we are introduced to the "author and perfecter" of the *new creation*, Jesus the Christ, who came to reclaim and redeem the world. As Moses was the first to pen God's story, so Mark became the first to record the story of Jesus, Son of God.

However, Moses and Mark are not just connected by the story they wrote and how they penned it. We see two other similarities in both their experience and condition that link them across the centuries.

Both men ran

Like John Mark, Moses ran away. He killed an Egyptian in defence of a fellow Hebrew and thought he had hidden his crime. The next day he tried to separate two Hebrews who were fighting only to be questioned:

"Who made you ruler and judge over us? Are you thinking of killing me as you killed the Egyptian?" (Exodus 2:14)

---

1. Some manuscripts do not have "Son of God". Mark is regarded by most NT scholars as the first of the four Gospels.

In fear, Moses ran for his life to the wilderness of Midian concluding, "What I did must have become known." (Exodus 2:14)

Both men had some form of physical impairment

Fast forward forty years and we see Moses shepherding in the "far side of the desert". The Lord called to him from a burning bush and commissioned him to return to Egypt to rescue His people. However, Moses used a number of excuses to push back on the Lord, one of which was his ability to speak:

"Moses said to the LORD, 'Pardon your servant, Lord. I have never been eloquent, neither in the past nor since you have spoken to your servant. I am slow of speech and tongue.'" (Exodus 4:10)

In the final phrase Moses wanted the Lord to know that he was "slow of speech and slow of tongue". The word translated "slow", used twice in the sentence is *kaḇēḏ*, which is used when describing something as "heavy, great or grievous", depending on the context. Moses had a "heavy tongue", hence the reason why most translations opt for "slow of tongue", and this has led some to suggest that Moses had some form of stammer or speech impediment.

As we move from Moses, take a closer look at John Mark. Notice the way he holds his quill. The shape of his fingers are unusual and he has adapted his writing style to accommodate the challenge, because John Mark was κολοβοδάκτυλος, meaning "stump-fingered"![2]

How wonderfully ironic, that the man who would become known as Moses the Teacher, and the author of the first five books of the Bible known as Torah, also had a *heavy tongue*, and that the first writer of the story of Jesus, whose work would inspire and assist other Gospel

2. Cross, F. L., & Livingstone, E. A. (Eds.). (2005). In *The Oxford dictionary of the Christian Church* (3rd ed. rev., p. 1045). Oxford; New York: Oxford University Press. The tradition that Mark was κολοβοδάκτυλος is found in the *Anti-Marcionite Prologues and in St *Hippolytus, *Haer*. 7. 30. Feast day, 25 Apr. κολοβος might suggest some form of stunted growth or even mutilation.

accounts, whose words have been read by billions of people, had *stump-fingers*. Both men not only wrote about a story of God's loving-kindness, faithfulness and grace, they lived it.

As we reflect on John Mark as the *stump-fingered storyteller*, his achievements serve as an inspiration to all recovering from failure, while facing the vulnerability of weakness and limitation. From his quill, John Mark speaks and encourages us with three great truths.

Impairment does not determine influence

One of the most inspirational books I have ever read is *Life Without Limits* by Nick Vujicic. The subtitle reads, *Inspiration for a Ridiculously Good Life*, and Nick seems to have just that. He has a beautiful wife, four children, is a world-renowned and much sought after speaker, a New York best-selling author, life coach and entrepreneur. What makes this all the more remarkable is that he was born without arms and legs. I've never had the privilege to hear any of his talks in person but I've watched him via media platforms and it is a truly mesmerising experience. It's humbling to hear a man speak with such passion about life, and to see that he has not allowed his obvious impairment to define or dictate to him. Rather, he has used his condition in a unique and exceptional way. His ambition is to "inspire and equip the world to know that we can all rise above adversity and overcome every disability of the heart and mind." This man and his message are well worth a moment of your time.[3]

The first time we are introduced to Barnabas it is using his birth name, not his apostolically given name:

"Joseph, a Levite from Cyprus, whom the apostles called Barnabas..." (Acts 4:36)

There is the possibility that if Joseph was a Levite, then as his relative, John Mark may have been from the same tribe. I am now in the world of conjecture, so I must be careful I don't build my house on sand, but

3. https://nickvujicic.com

in the light of his condition, it is worthy of consideration. As a tribe, the Levites were "set apart" unto the Lord and took the place of the "firstborn" who belonged to the Lord.[4] Within the tribe there were three family clans, Gershon, Kohath and Merari, with the priests coming from Kohath. Thus, all priests were Levites but not all Levites could be priests. The Levites served the Lord by supporting the priests and by carrying out various duties around the Tabernacle and later the Temple. It was their job to help the people to worship the Lord and fulfil the requirements of the Law in that regard.

Was John Mark a Levite?

In truth, we don't know, but if he was, even if he was from the Kohath clan, he could never have served as a priest, according to the guidelines contained in Leviticus:

"Say to Aaron: 'For the generations to come none of your descendants who has a *defect* may come near to offer the food of his God. No man who has any *defect* may come near: no man who is blind or lame, disfigured or deformed; no man with a crippled foot or hand, or who is a hunchback or a dwarf, or who has any eye defect, or who has festering or running sores or damaged testicles. No descendant of Aaron the priest who has any *defect* is to come near to present the food offerings to the Lord. He has a *defect*; he must not come near to offer the food of his God. He may eat the most holy food of his God, as well as the holy food; yet because of his *defect*, he must not go near the curtain or approach the altar, and so desecrate My sanctuary. I am the LORD, who makes them holy. '" (Leviticus 21:17-23)[5]

From our 21st century viewpoint, these words will be seen as outdated and discriminatory against people with disability, with no less than five references to "defect". But we must remember that these requirements

4. Numbers 3:41
5. It is not completely clear if these requirements were only for the Priests or applied in general to all Levites who served.

were only for a specific group of people, fulfilling a specific function, for a specific reason. This passage should not be read as God's view of people with disability, but rather an indication of His place of holiness, perfection and set-apartness. This is about *His* distinctiveness, not human discrimination.[6]

With "stump-fingers" John Mark may have known the pain of exclusion and the sting of superficial judgement. Some may have looked at his hands and changed their view of him, deciding what he could or could not be. The Priest's hands that offered the "bread of the Lord" in the Tabernacle or Temple had to be without defect, but the Lord chose John Mark as His *first* to offer the *bread of His Word* to the world. The fingers that penned, "The beginning of the gospel of Jesus Christ, Son of God", were themselves symbols of the grace, inclusion and redemptive power of His glorious gospel, and those words written by John Mark's impaired fingers continue to influence billions of people across the earth. We are all impaired in one way or another, with some facing greater challenges than others, but our limitations need not define us nor our impairment diminish us.

There are opportunities in the obstacles

The prisoner barracks at the Ravensbruck Nazi concentration camp were both overcrowded and flea invested. This was home for Corrie ten Boom and her sister, Betsy, who as followers of Jesus had miraculously managed to smuggle a Bible into the camp. As they read the Scriptures together, it encouraged them to give thanks in all things and that the Lord could use anything for good. Betsy decided that this meant thanking God for the fleas! Corrie was repulsed by the idea but upon Betsy's insistence, she also thanked God for the fleas.

---

6. mûm: This word usually describes a physical characteristic that is deemed to be bad. The same idea was applied to animals being brought for sacrifice, Lev. 22:20, 21; Num. 19:2; Deut. 17:1.

Over the next few months they realised that the guards did not enter their barracks, which not only gave them relief from being assaulted by the guards, but in their absence they were able to hold open Bible studies and prayer meetings without interference. Through this, many women came to faith in Jesus. Only at the end did they discover why the guards had left them alone. It was because of the fleas! Thank God for the fleas.[7]

Sometimes what looks like an obstacle can lead to an opportunity. Paul experienced this when he tried to visit the believers at Thessalonica.

"For we wanted to come to you – certainly I, Paul, did, again and again – but Satan blocked our way." (1 Thessalonians 2:18)

Paul claimed that Satan *cut in* on him, so that he could not do what he wanted to do. So what was his response to such an obstacle that refused to move? When he couldn't do what he wanted to do, he did what he could do! Two dynamic opportunities were created because of the way Paul responded to this obstacle.

Opportunity #1: Paul sent Timothy

"...we were willing to be left behind at Athens alone, and we sent Timothy... to establish and exhort you in your faith." (1 Thessalonians 3:1-2)

Timothy got sent because Paul got stopped. Later Timothy, one of Paul's sons, would emerge as one of the foremost leaders in the church at Ephesus, so this became an opportunity to shine, showing both his worth and his growth. Approximately five years later, Paul had a similar experience while in prison, from where he wrote to the church at Philippi:

"I want you to know, brothers, that what has happened to me has really served to advance the gospel..." (Philippians 1:12)

---

7. James Emery White blog, *Church and Culture*, 25th November 2021, quoting *The Hiding Place* by Corrie ten Boom.

The word translated advance is *prokoptō*, meaning "to forward cut", which is a lovely contrast on the idea stated to the Thessalonians when Paul spoke of Satan *cutting in* on him (*egkóptō*). Paul learned that the Lord could find a way to cut forward and forge a new path, even when Satan or the circumstances of life cut in against him and try to stop his progress. As the work advanced with Timothy at Thessalonica, so it advanced in prison, even though Paul was in chains.

"...it has become clear throughout the whole palace guard and to everyone that I am in chains for Christ. Because of my chains, most of the brothers in the Lord have been encouraged to speak the word of God more courageously and fearlessly." (Philippians 1:13-14)

Paul found an opportunity in the obstacle. When he couldn't do what he wanted to do, he did what he could do.

Opportunity #2: Paul wrote a letter

Instead of going to them, Paul was forced to write to them, a letter we now have in the New Testament called 1 Thessalonians.

"I charge you before the Lord to have this letter read to all the brothers and sisters." (5:27)

Paul wrote this letter to the Thessalonians from a place of restriction, unable to go where he wanted to go. We continue to be enriched today by this wonderful letter, written by Paul around 50/51AD, because he did what he could do. As we look at the New Testament as a whole, Paul authored thirteen letters/books and at least four of them were written from prison, namely, Ephesians, Philippians, Colossians and Philemon. All of these are rich, multi-layered masterpieces that have kept theologians occupied for 2000 years and inspired the Christian community to live for Jesus; and all of them were opportunities found amidst obstacles. It seems Paul's obstacles were a catalyst for innovation.[8]

8. The 13 letters do not include Hebrews and some scholars believe that 1 Thessalonians was written from Paul's imprisonment at Ephesus.

Paul found an opportunity in the obstacle. When he couldn't do what he wanted to do, he did what he could do.

Did John Mark learn from Paul in this regard? Reflecting on the potential obstacle of John Mark's disability, H.B. Swete concluded,

"Such a defect, to whatever cause it was due, may have helped to mould the course of John Mark's life; by closing against him a more ambitious career, it may have turned his thoughts to those secondary ministries, for which he was perhaps naturally fitted… 'Mark the stump-fingered' has rendered enduring services to the Church, which, in the absence of such an infirmity, it might never have been his lot to undertake."[9]

Could it be that John Mark's obstacle became, in God, an opportunity? Maybe the Lord was able to use his stump-fingers to get John Mark to where He wanted him to go.

In 1982 I had a simple plan. At sixteen I was going to join the Royal Ulster Constabulary cadets (RUC), then at eighteen become a full-time police officer. When I was twenty-one, I would leave for England to join the Paratroopers and hopefully go to officer school and see the world (oh, and not get killed in the process).[10] My father knew a recruiting officer for the RUC and when he heard I was applying, he was delighted, assuring my dad that, "The RUC needs young men like your John."

However, with over 625 applicants and the Cadets only offering 25 spaces, we all knew that only *the best* would get in. After my medical, I discovered that I was not among the best. Due to a weakness in my left eye, which I never knew I had, my masterplan came crashing down. I was heartbroken. The Lord had failed me. This was my plan and it was a good one. However, within months of my rejection, I had an encounter

---

9. www.biblicalstudies.org.uk, an article by H.B.Swete.
Swete, H. B. (Ed.). (1898). *The Gospel according to St. Mark. The Greek text with introduction, notes and indices* (p. xxvii). London; New York: MacMillan and co.; The MacMillan Company.
10. Today the police force of Northern Ireland is PSNI, Police Service of Northern Ireland. The name was changed in 2001.

with the Lord that changed the direction of my life. Instead of the police academy I found myself in a Bible college and instead of the battlefield, I got to see the world through a pulpit.

Had I got my way, survived the Troubles and joined the Army, by my retirement age of 55 (provided I stayed alive), I would potentially have experienced in one form or another no fewer than 10 conflicts across the globe. I would have seen the world alright, but not in the way I should have.

To this day I thank the Lord for my weak eye. My obstacle, so horrible at the time, became an opportunity for something bigger, greater and better. There are moments when obstacles are our friends, and for me, this was surely one of them.

Is there an opportunity lurking in your obstacle?

Could it be that the restriction you're experiencing might be the catalyst for innovation?

Is perhaps your disappointment in not being able to do what you want to do, distracting you from something you might be able to do?

Why not surrender the obstacle to the Lord and ask Him for eyes to see the opportunity before you.

His wonder can be displayed through our weakness

In Acts 18 we read that Paul arrived in Corinth after his experience at the Areopagus in Athens. Leaving chapter 17 and moving into chapter 18, it looks like business as usual for the apostle and his team. But later, when he wrote to the church he helped establish through that visit, we get an insight into how the man of God felt.

"When I came to you, brothers, I did not come with eloquence or superior wisdom… I came to you in weakness and fear, and with much trembling."

He concluded,

"My message and my preaching were not with wise and persuasive words, but with the demonstration of the Spirit's power, so that your faith might not rest on men's wisdom, but on God's power." (1 Corinthians 2:1-5)

This might reflect that Paul was less than pleased with the outcome of his trip to Athens, during which he tried to engage with the local intellectual community through argument. Some believe that Paul's sermon at Mars Hill is a brilliant example of contextual preaching, while others feel Paul moved away from the foundational core of his appeal through Jesus. However we conclude and whatever Paul felt, it is clear he arrived in Corinth with less confidence in his own eloquence and more in the power of the Spirit.

This might explain Paul's passionate defence of the "foolishness" of the message of the cross and the community redeemed by Jesus' death:

"Brothers and sisters, think of what you were when you were called. Not many of you were wise by human standards; not many were influential; not many were of noble birth. But God chose the foolish things of the world to shame the wise; God chose the weak things of the world to shame the strong. God chose the lowly things of this world and the despised things – and the things that are not – to nullify the things that are, so that no one may boast before him. It is because of him that you are in Christ Jesus, who has become for us wisdom from God – that is, our righteousness, holiness and redemption. Therefore, as it is written: 'Let the one who boasts boast in the Lord.'" (1 Corinthians 1:26-31)

Look at the contrast and juxtaposition of Paul's language:

"...not many were *wise*... not many were *influential*, (the word is *dunatós* pointing more toward being strong and powerful)... not many were of *noble* birth..."

Having established what many *were not*, he celebrated what God can do through the *foolish*, *weak* and *ignoble*.

"foolish... to shame the wise."[11]

"weak... to shame the strong."[12]

"lowly... and despised... the things that are not... to nullify the things that are."[13]

But why does the Lord do this and why does He work this way?

Paul gives us the answer:

"...so that no one may boast before Him... 'Let the one who boasts, boast in the Lord.'" (1 Corinthians 1:29 and 31)

John Mark is a glorious example of this idea at work. Viewed by many of his contemporaries as foolish for taking up the cause of Jesus the Messiah, his story is not only one of weakness, and to some extent ignominy, but of recovery, restoration and redemption. The *unfit* had become *useful*, the *under-rower* a *fellow-worker*, and the *deserter* a man of trustworthiness and influence. His foolish words would shame the wise, his weakness would confound the strong and his lowliness would render ineffective the social, economic and political barriers that stood in the way of the spread of the Gospel across the Roman Empire. The words penned by the stump-fingered author would penetrate to the heart of Rome, outlast its reign, and help establish a Kingdom community, bigger than anything Caesar could have dreamed or imagined.

The Lord is drawn to our weakness, not because He delights in our vulnerability but so that He can come to us, work in us and demonstrate through us His glory, majesty and power. Weakness without the Lord is debilitating, but weakness with the Lord is liberating. Weakness without the Lord makes us vulnerable, but weakness with the Lord empowers us to victory. Paul understood that the Lord's grace was sufficient and

---

11. *mōrós*; silly, stupid, foolish, from which the English word moron is derived.
12. *asthenḗs*; without strength, powerless. Weak, powerless, without physical ability.
13. *agenḗs*; ignoble, one who does not live up to the expectation of his stock, race or nation. It is found only in 1 Corinthians 1:28. *Exoutheneṓ*; to bring to naught. To despise, treat with scorn.

that His power was made complete in his weakness, hence the reason he could confidently declare,

"Therefore I will boast all the more gladly about my weaknesses, so that Christ's power may rest on me. That is why, for Christ's sake, I delight in weaknesses, in insults, in hardships, in persecutions, in difficulties. For when I am weak, then I am strong." (2 Corinthians 12:9-10)

When it says, "I delight in weaknesses", though I like this translation, the word has more intentionality implied within it and becomes even stronger. The word is *eudokéō* and could literally be translated "to think good or well". Thus, when Paul delights, this is not his dynamic personality kicking in but rather a mind trained and transformed by divine truth that teaches weakness is better than strength!

As John Mark's quill scratches across the parchment, held by stump-fingers, he reminds us that our impairment does not determine our influence, that opportunities are often hidden in the obstacles, and that God's wonder can be displayed in and through our weakness.

Whoever you are and wherever you are, it's time to *pick up your quill and write*!

Time for Reflection

As we reflect on John Mark as the *stump-fingered storyteller*, his achievements serve as an inspiration to all recovering from failure, while facing the vulnerability of weakness and limitation.

Impairment does not determine influence

What truths can help transform something that limits us, to become something that can bear influence for the glory of God? How might *we* need to change in order for *it* to change?

There are opportunities in the obstacles

Could it be that the restriction you are experiencing might be the catalyst for innovation? Is it possible to surrender the fight against the obstacle in pursuit of a God-created opportunity?

As you look back on your life, have you discovered that some obstacles were actually life-saving opportunities?

His wonder can be displayed in our weakness

Why do we struggle with the idea of our weakness being a vehicle for the Lord's strength?

10. Leading the Way

"Very truly I tell you, unless a kernel of wheat falls to the ground and dies, it remains only a single seed. But if it dies, it produces many seeds. Anyone who loves their life will lose it, while anyone who hates their life in this world will keep it for eternal life."
(Jesus the Christ, Son of God)[1]

I am writing this final chapter from the study in my home. Dawn and I feel extraordinarily blessed to live where we live and have the home we have. We love it here and our prayer is that all those who visit us will experience both the Lord's *shuv*, His restorative power, and *shalom*, the peace that only He can give. Many times people have commented on how "pretty" the exterior of our home looks and every time I smile a smile that I think John Mark would understand. Our home is dressed with reclaimed bricks. The beauty people see are bricks that have been rescued from old buildings, cleaned up and reused. Some of our bricks have edges that are worn and irregular, while others are marked and discoloured. Yet, having been given a second chance, they come together and form something that is not only practical, but pleasing to the eye.

The greatest sign that we are grateful for a second chance is a life well-lived. Not everyone who gets a second chance takes it, but this was certainly not the case for John Mark. Looking at him now, the *son* and *scribe* of Peter, the *fellow-worker* of Paul, the *friend* of Luke and the *storyteller* of Jesus, it is easy to be captivated by the beauty we see. However, we must not make the mistake of being so enamoured by the product that we ignore the process that helped produce it. John Mark, a *reclaimed brick* with his chequered history and stump-fingers, found

1. John 12:24-25

his place in a building full of bricks just like him, declaring the glory of God's grace.

But we haven't finished with his story just yet. Christian history and tradition suggests three more insights about John Mark that are worthy of our consideration, even if we handle some of those considerations with care.[2]

He led the way in mission – from Jerusalem to regions beyond

Some believe that John Mark was a native of North Africa and that he was born in the city of Cyrene in Pentapolis, in Libya.[3] We know from the book of Acts that his family had clearly relocated to Israel and were living in Jerusalem. John Mark liked his home in Jerusalem, having returned there from Perga when he left Barnabas and Paul. When we reflected on John Mark's desertion back in chapter three, there was a suggestion that although he may have run out of fear, his return to Jerusalem may have also been due to Paul's attitude to, and comfort with, the Gentiles – something that John Mark was not ready to embrace. But as we follow his journey, we observe him in Cyprus with Barnabas, Rome with Peter, and a return to his home of North Africa in general and Egypt in particular, to proclaim the good news of Jesus. He did not only go full circle on his geographical journey, but moved dramatically in both his theology and missiology. Having left Jerusalem he embraced the Gentile world.

A second chance usually demands change, whether it be in our attitudes, beliefs, actions or relationships. A moment of failure will always cause us to see the world differently, the key is whether we see it

2. There are various views believed about John Mark (St. Mark) by different streams within Christendom. The credibility and validity of some of these ideas are the subject of ongoing debate.
3. https://www.copticchurch.net/synaxarium/saints/mark.html

out of the pain it caused or the change it provoked. One of the potential benefits of failure is that it grants us the opportunity to look again at what we believe, why we believe it, and what that belief is producing. It gives us the chance to examine our drivers, our priorities and our relationships, to see if they are good for our souls and fit for purpose. John Mark not only fell down in Paul's eyes but was deemed unfit for the type of service on offer: going to Gentile communities and offering them the good news of Jesus. However, John Mark learned from his fall and he changed in the rejection. As a result, he was able to go to places that previously may have seemed improbable if not impossible to him.

He led the way in ministry - from fellow-worker to shepherd

John Mark is accepted across many streams within Christendom as the founder of the Alexandrian Church.[4] Having been "the first to set out to Egypt to preach the gospel" he became the bishop or shepherd to the Christian community there.[5]

Alexandria was founded by Alexander the Great in 331BC and was formally brought under Roman rule in 30BC. With both its strategic position and great harbour, Alexandria had developed into an influential trading centre where East met West, holding the key to the Egyptian granary, which Rome became increasingly reliant upon. It was a powerhouse for science, literature, mathematics and philosophy, as well as being home to a large and thriving Jewish community, forming a major centre for Jewish learning. It was in Alexandria that the Septuagint

4. Swete, H. B. (Ed.). (1898). *The Gospel according to St. Mark. The Greek text with introduction, notes and indices* (p. xviii). London; New York: The MacMillan Company.
5. Eusebius of Caesarea, a Roman historian referred to as the "first church historian" and also as the "father of Church History" (Doergen 1937:446-448; cf. Verdoner 2014:239) wrote a ten-volume work called Historia Ecclesiastica in the 4th century - between 300 and 325 CE.

was produced, the Greek translation of the Hebrew Scriptures (Old Testament).[6] By the time of Augustus[7] the city walls encompassed an area of 5.34 km^2 with a growing and diverse population within.[8]

So much within his background equipped John Mark for the day he arrived in the city. As a writer and scholar with a Jewish heritage, and missional world view that embraced Gentiles, John Mark would surely have loved Alexandria as a city offering spectacular opportunity. Having served with Barnabas, Peter and Paul, he would have witnessed the establishment of many Christian communities in numerous great cities across the Roman world. All his learning, experience and training culminated for him in Alexandria where he helped build a thriving and influential church. As the Lighthouse of Alexandria (one of the seven wonders of the Ancient world) cast its light far and wide, so under the shepherding care of John Mark, the light of the Gospel shone forth, influencing the region for centuries to come.

A second chance often creates an opportunity for growth. In the aftermath of failure we can discover things about ourselves that we did not realise were there and we might find gifts and talents emerge out of us, released from their dormancy by a season of crisis and change. John Mark's trajectory of growth had taken him from *under-rower* to *fellow-worker* and to *shepherd*. This should not be seen as a progression up the ladder of his career, but rather a journey deeper in the heart of service. John Mark had grown from a somewhat selfish young man to a selfless shepherd, prepared to give the best of his life to the service of Jesus and His Church.

---

6. https://www.britannica.com/place/Alexandria-Egypt/History
7. Augustus reigned 63BC - 14AD
8. Delia, Diana (1988). "*The Population of Roman Alexandria*". Transactions of the American Philological Association. Vol.118: 275–292, https://www.jstor.org

He led the way in martyrdom – from deserter to martyr

For first century followers of The Way, martyrdom was not just a possibility, it was a reality. Helped by biblical record and church history, we know that of the original twelve disciples that Jesus called (excluding Judas), only John escaped martyrdom. His was the privilege of torture and exile! John Mark was not the first follower of Jesus to die at the hands of an angry mob and he would not be the last. The Coptic Church, who regard St. Mark (John Mark) as both their founder and first great Patriarch, claim that he was martyred in 68AD when the "pagans of Serapis, tied him to a horse's tail and dragged him through the streets of Alexandria's district of Bokalia for two days until his body was torn to pieces."[9]

However John Mark died, his death was not in vain. As Jesus Himself said:

"Very truly I tell you, unless a kernel of wheat falls to the ground and dies, it remains only a single seed. But if it dies, it produces many seeds." (John 12:24)

Just as Jesus before him had surrendered to the purpose of the Father and given His life so lavishly for the salvation of the world, so in death, John Mark's life was transformed from a "single seed" (it abides alone) to "many seeds" (bears much fruit). Previously John Mark, in an act of self-love, had tried to save his life by deserting his friends, but now years later he understood that the best way to have eternal life was to "hate" his own.[10] John Mark learned to shun the temptation to be the master of his own destiny and realised that his life belonged to someone else and his purpose to a higher calling.

---

9. https://www.suscopts.org/coptic-orthodox/church/saint-mark/
https://www.copticchurch.net/synaxarium/saints/mark.html
10. The use of the word hate (*miséo*) is being used idiomatically as in other parts of Jesus' teaching. Jesus is not encouraging self-hate, but rather to love ourselves less when compared to our love for Him.

A second chance is an invitation to learn. My granny used to say that "we live and learn", but I have found that is not always the case. Matthew Syed argues that "...failure to learn from mistakes has been one of the greatest single obstacles to human progress."[11] Over the years I've observed in myself and others a reluctance to learn, which in turn produces a resistance to growth and an obstacle to change. This lack of learning condemns us to making the same mistakes over and over again. Our experiences, whether they be good, bad or ugly, have no power to teach us anything, rather it is our response to such moments, our openness in the aftermath of failure, and our humility in the light of crisis that will lead us to learning and life. If our failure is seen (by us and/or others) as terminal, then the only thing we can learn from it is how to die. But if we can redefine failure, we can "unleash progress, creativity and resilience."[12]

As we approach the end of our journey together with John Mark, there are three final things I want to highlight and celebrate before leaving you and him. The golden thread of these ideas can be identified through the pages of this book but they are worthy of one final mention. In celebrating the fall and rise of John Mark it is important to remember...

The Goodness of friends

Solomon wrote,

"If one falls down his friend can help him up. But pity the man who falls and has no-one to help him up." (Ecclesiastes 4:10)

The second part of this verse, if read more literally, says:

"But woe to him that is *alone* (or is one) when he falls..."

John Mark made it because he was not alone, or one on his own. Though we have not made much of it, there is no doubt in my mind that when he returned to Jerusalem, his godly mother would have ensured

---

11. Syed, M., *Black Box Thinking*, John Murray Publishing, UK, 2016, p.12
12. Syed, *Black Box Thinking*, p.14

that having fallen down he did not stay down. However, we do know that Barnabas *took him*, Peter *fathered him* and eventually Paul *supported*, *endorsed* and *released him*. John Mark did not rise on his own, but rather he was able to rise because good, faithful, generous people stood with him and refused to let him die.

There are numerous unsung heroes of the Christian faith who have stepped into the world of a *John Mark* and refused to leave until the job was done. They have prayed, listened, challenged, wept, served and persevered when the rest of the world stopped caring and moved on. There are vibrant marriages, strong ministries and celebrated individuals who would not be here if it had not been for the commitment of good friends.

If you are one of those unsung heroes, I salute you. I thank God for you and I want to tell you that the Lord is "...not unjust; He will not forget your work and the love you have shown Him as you have helped His people and continue to help them."[13]

If you have been a *John Mark* and you know you would not have made it without the help of good friends, then I urge you, remember them, honour them, celebrate them and, if you can, bless them. You get to look good because they refused to give up. Let your success be theirs and let your life be a reminder of how amazing they are!

In celebrating the fall and rise of John Mark it is important to remember...

The Grit of John Mark

The Winged Lion is accepted by many within Christendom as the symbol of St. Mark the Evangelist and there are various reasons why (some biblical and others more mythical) this image represents John

13. Hebrews 6:10

Mark.[14] Although I'm not drawn to such iconography, I would venture to suggest my own interpretation of the Winged Lion in the light of our journey with John Mark.

Isaiah wrote:

"But those who hope in the LORD will renew their strength. They will soar on wings like eagles; they will run and not grow weary, they will walk and not be faint." (Isaiah 40:31)

Those who hope in the Lord... get wings.

The word translated "hope" is *qāwāh*, and the root meaning is that of "twisting or winding a strand of cord or rope". I love the idea that hope happens when we get twisted into the Lord; when like a rope our cord is empowered by His. John Mark found hope in the Lord. In the darkness of his failure and in the despair that must have accompanied this event, he learned to twist himself into the Lord and allowed the Lord's strength to become his. The strength John Mark found as he hoped in the Lord gave him wings to fly again!

Solomon declared:

"The wicked man flees though no one pursues, but the righteous are as bold as a lion." (Proverbs 28:1)

John Mark did flee but he returned, and having returned he stuck with the task until the very end. He showed the boldness (not arrogance) of a lion in taking the second chance offered to him, and even in the face of rejection by Paul he refused to run away again. John Mark displayed that boldness in serving Barnabas, scribing for Peter, working with Paul and going all the way to Alexandria and North Africa. He expressed that boldness when his stump-fingers picked up the quill to write the good news of Jesus and he showed that boldness when the mob attacked him and dragged him to his death.

---

14. Some point to both Ezekiel 1:10 and Revelation 4:7 and the four "living creatures" around the throne. Mark as the Lion, Matthew as the human, Luke as the Ox and John as the Eagle.

John Mark... the Winged Lion!

In failure it is easy to believe that hope has gone and boldness could never return. But John Mark shows us that it is possible; to once again live in the boldness that hope in the Lord gives. There are no short-cuts and easy answers, but if we are willing to twist ourselves into the Lord and take hold of what He puts in front of us, then like John Mark, we too could soar like a winged lion. Our hope does not come from positivity and our boldness from our personality, but rather we recognise that our hope comes from His presence and our boldness from His promises. If John Mark can fly again, so can we!

In celebrating the fall and rise of John Mark it is important to remember...

The Grace of God

When Jesus lived on earth His job was as a *téktōn*. This has generally been translated as a "carpenter", but in the context of His world, Jesus was probably a craftsman able to work not only with wood but stone as well. The word from which we get our English word architect is *architéktōn*, and points to the idea of being a master builder. I love the thought that Jesus the master builder took the rejected stone of John Mark and with His hands of grace and skill, patiently trimmed and cut, thus ensuring this stone could be reused. As the "Living Stone", Jesus knew the pain of rejection only to be repositioned to become the "precious cornerstone", and having been rejected by "the builders", He became "the capstone."[15]

I'm so glad I serve a God who does not abandon the "works of His hands." He has promised "never to leave us and never to forsake us". David declared,

"For great is Your loving-kindness, reaching to the heavens; your faithfulness reaches to the skies." (Psalm 57:10)

15. 1 Peter 2:4-8

As the Lord spoke to His people through Isaiah, He reminded them,

"See, I have engraved you on the palms of My hands; your walls are ever before Me."

Our names are *cut into* the hands of the Lord. He cannot forget us... He will not forget us. I have been able to tell the story of John Mark primarily because of the grace of God. Without that generous gift of His goodness, faithfulness and love, John Mark would have been lost, a footnote in the history of the Church; a story of the boy that could have been, should have been and might have been. But because of God's grace, John Mark did not disappear into infamy, rather he rose as one reclaimed, restored and re-commissioned.

Even when the goodness of friends runs thin and our grit and determination runs low, the grace of the Lord will never run out. He is the God of the *second chance.* He loves us... He is for us... He is with us... and if we let Him, He can shape us for His purpose and use us for His glory.

Time for Reflection

The greatest sign that we are grateful for a second chance is a life well lived. A second chance usually demands change.

If we want a different outcome, then we cannot stay the same. What needs to change in our beliefs and behaviour to make the most of a second chance?

A second chance often creates an opportunity for growth. In what areas do we need to grow to make the most of a second chance? How can we be more intentional in the development of the gifts we have been given?

A second chance is an invitation to learn. From whom can we learn, what can we learn, and how can we learn in order to make the most of a second chance?

About the Author

John has been in full-time Church leadership since 1987. Though called to the UK, John has ministered in almost 40 nations of the world. Based in his local church, New Life Church, Scunthorpe, he has authored fifteen books and currently serves on the Apostolic Team of One Church Gloucester and its wider network, while also being released to teach in a wider translocal context. As a leader, teacher and author John has a passion to equip and inspire leaders, as well as empower followers of Jesus into effective lifestyle and service.

For more information visit:
www.drjohnandrews.co.uk

By the Same Author

The power of Sabbath-centric living

Author John Andrews challenges us to look at our lives in the light of Adam and Eve's "first day" on the planet. Although the Sabbath was "day 7" for God in terms of creation, it was "day 1" for newly created humanity. Before God asked Adam and Eve to "do" anything, He invited them simply to "be" - to enjoy and understand the power of rest.

What happened to Jesus during His 'silent years'?

As Jesus is about to enter into eighteen years of obscurity, Luke gives us only one clue as to His preoccupation during those years, informing us, "Jesus grew in wisdom and stature, and in favour with God and man" (Luke 2:52). The temptation is to think that Jesus grew "naturally" in these areas, but the verse implies that He grew intentionally, *on purpose*. Every follower of Jesus has to learn to "lead themselves" before they lead others. Contained in 2:52 is the vital blueprint we must follow.

It's time to start thinking inside the box!

We've all heard of "thinking outside the box" and "limitless living" to achieve our "full potential", but what if we're not supposed to think "outside the box"? What if the idea of life without limits is a myth? – one that will trap us and leave us unfulfilled, confused and frustrated? Discover the joy of living your life in the "box" of purpose, tailor-made for you by God.

By the Same Author

The story of a woman whose actions can only be described as *extravagant*

Explore the story of the woman who speaks not one word in the New Testament account, but whose actions proclaim a message, loud and clear to us all. She risked what little reputation she had to minister to Jesus in an unforgettable way in the worst possible context. As we look beneath the surface, her expression of worship is more shocking and more glorious that we first realise.

Everyone gets broken at some point. But how do we find power in that pain?

Brokenness is a reality that every follower of Jesus will experience at some point on their journey. In those moments of trial, pain, fear or failure we look to the Lord for rescue and deliverance. We're grateful for the times He saves us *from* the valley, but what of the moments when we experience His salvation by walking with Him *through* the valley?

"God is Love!"

The last three words of 1 John 4:8 form one of the most profound, amazing statements in the whole Bible. For many, they are also the hardest to believe. The most important thing a person can know is the truth that, *You are loved*. God knew exactly how much loving you would cost, and He was willing to pay whatever price had to be paid. Do you know how much you are worth to Him?

By the Same Author

The tyranny of pretence will leave us exhausted, frustrated and disappointed, as we attempt to sustain a person we were never meant to be. But a face to face encounter with God will change everything...

"John's message of the absolute necessity of living authentically, free from pretence, with integrity, vulnerability and openness is one our generation is craving to hear. This is a thoroughly Bible-centred book. Read it, look for His face and listen for His voice." – **Steve Campbell, Senior Pastor, C3 Church**

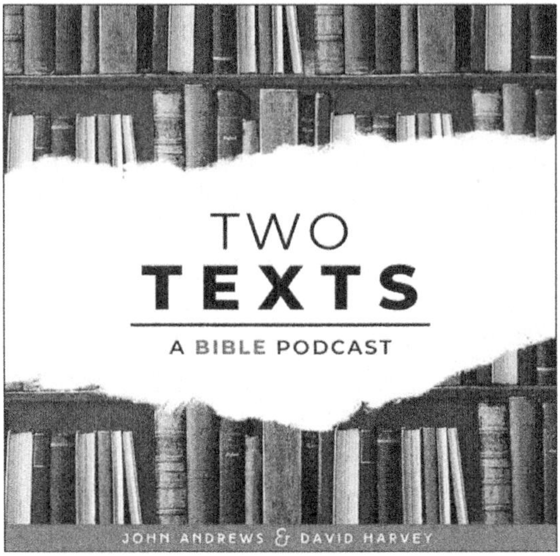

Two Texts – A Bible Podcast

Every two weeks, from two different countries, the two hosts of the Two Texts podcast pick two biblical texts to talk about.

Dr John Andrews and Dr David Harvey share a mutual fascination with the Bible. Simple yet complex; ancient yet relevant; challenging yet comforting. But one thing that fascinates them consistently is that, like a kaleidoscope, no matter how many times they look at it there is something new, fresh and exciting to talk about.

This podcast is designed for you regardless of how much or how little you've read the Bible. Grab a hot beverage, a notepad (or app), and a Bible, sit back, listen, enjoy, and learn to also become fascinated (or grow your fascination) with this exciting, compelling and mysterious book.